# Victorian Roses

MORE EMBROIDERY
AND PASTIMES
FOR THE 21ST CENTURY

*Dedicated to Sam,*
*my daughter, and Hans,*
*my colleague and balance,*
*and to my friends*
*and protectors;*
*thank you for coming*
*into my life.*
*And in loving memory*
*of Ezzie.*

First published in 2000 for
Quilters' Resource Inc.
P.O. Box 148850
Chicago, IL 60614
Phone 773 278-5695

Designer: Suzy King
Photography: Simon Blackall
Styling: Jenny Haskins
Printed and bound in China

Library of Congress
Cataloguing-in Publication Data

Haskins, Jenny
Victorian Roses : more embroidery and pastimes for the 21st century
ISBN 1 - 889682 - 15 - 2

# Victorian Roses

MORE EMBROIDERY
AND PASTIMES
FOR THE 21ST CENTURY

*Jenny Haskins*

Quilters' Resource publications

# Contents

# Introduction

To create a book with a theme of Victorian roses seemed a natural step from *Victorian Pansies*, as both these flowers embody the essence of the Victorian era. So it is with great enthusiasm that we present this second book in the Victorian trilogy.

The rose, the Queen of Flowers, with its flounce of petals, profusion of blooms, harmonious color and lingering perfume always casts a spell. Just say the word and the image and mystique instantly come to mind. And when a rose is gone, its memory lingers on. Words, however extravagant, can never really capture the pure beauty of color and substance that is a rose.

Throughout history the rose has stood for romance, constancy, war, secrecy and valor. Its shape, color and the formation of its petals have been a constant delight, challenging the artist to capture the beauty of the sweet buds and blooms.

Roses have long been my favorite flowers inspiring first my hand-sewing needle, then my artist's brush and more recently my sewing machine with all its creative technological power. For long I have dreamt of replicating hand embroidery by machine, so it seemed only natural that I progress from painting an image to transforming it into wonderful machine embroidered roses that rival handwork and can be made by everyone, whatever their level of expertise.

So it is with *Victorian Roses* when a strip of leftover fabric, as if by magic, is turned into a purse of such breath-taking beauty that even the most reticent will be inspired to embrace the wonderful world of machine embroidery. Afternoon tea parties, lace shawls, cushions in all shapes and sizes, slippers, a jacket, a silken christening robe, quilt, hat, hat box, a pompadour lady, pin cushions, magnificent embroidery by hand and machine all tumble from

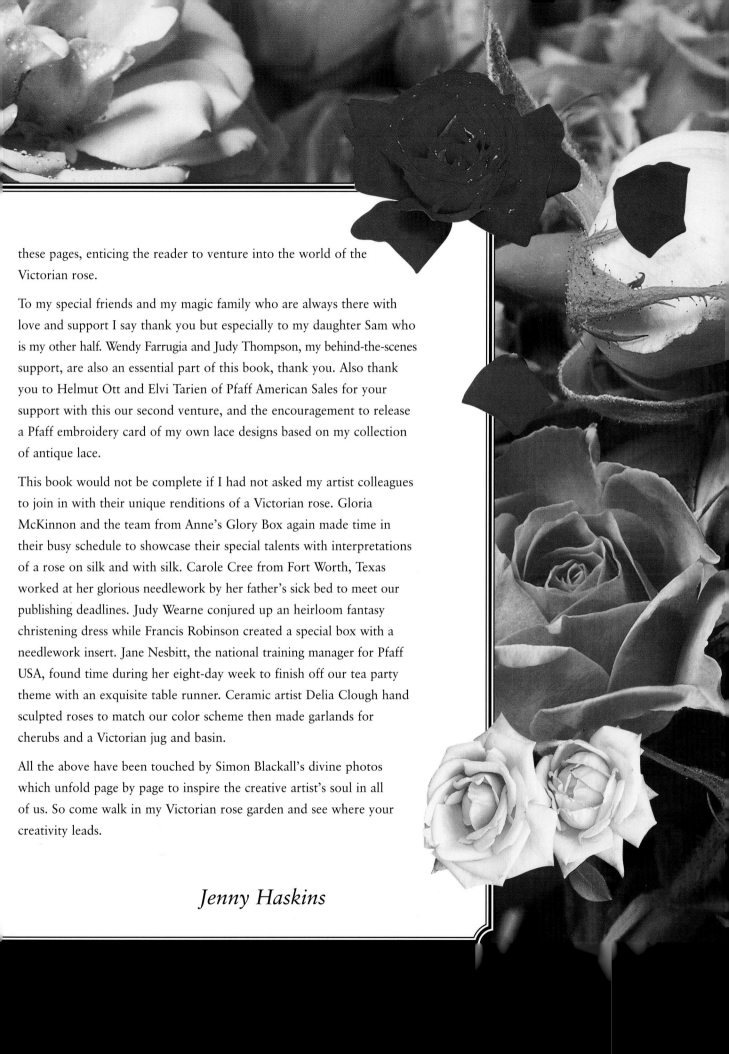

these pages, enticing the reader to venture into the world of the Victorian rose.

To my special friends and my magic family who are always there with love and support I say thank you but especially to my daughter Sam who is my other half. Wendy Farrugia and Judy Thompson, my behind-the-scenes support, are also an essential part of this book, thank you. Also thank you to Helmut Ott and Elvi Tarien of Pfaff American Sales for your support with this our second venture, and the encouragement to release a Pfaff embroidery card of my own lace designs based on my collection of antique lace.

This book would not be complete if I had not asked my artist colleagues to join in with their unique renditions of a Victorian rose. Gloria McKinnon and the team from Anne's Glory Box again made time in their busy schedule to showcase their special talents with interpretations of a rose on silk and with silk. Carole Cree from Fort Worth, Texas worked at her glorious needlework by her father's sick bed to meet our publishing deadlines. Judy Wearne conjured up an heirloom fantasy christening dress while Francis Robinson created a special box with a needlework insert. Jane Nesbitt, the national training manager for Pfaff USA, found time during her eight-day week to finish off our tea party theme with an exquisite table runner. Ceramic artist Delia Clough hand sculpted roses to match our color scheme then made garlands for cherubs and a Victorian jug and basin.

All the above have been touched by Simon Blackall's divine photos which unfold page by page to inspire the creative artist's soul in all of us. So come walk in my Victorian rose garden and see where your creativity leads.

*Jenny Haskins*

## GENERAL SEWING REQUIREMENTS

- Pfaff 7570 sewing machine and the Creative Fantasy embroidery unit
- Pfaff PC-Designer Software and/or Card Station
- Pfaff Creative cards
- Pfaff Fantasy embroidery cards
- Jenny Haskins Pfaff Choice card
- Victorian Roses design disk by Jenny Haskins
- Victorian Bows and Butterflies signature disk by Jenny Haskins with Cactus Punch
- Machine feet: open-toe foot, normal sewing foot, ¼-inch foot, zipper foot, narrow edge foot, and clear-view freehand foot
- Machine needles: size-80 embroidery needle, size-75 universal, and size-60 sharp
- Pre-wound embroidery bobbins
- Madeira rayon 40 embroidery thread
- Monofilament thread
- Metallic thread
- Self-adhesive tear-away stabilizer
- Water-soluble fabric stabilizer
- Photocopy paper stabilizer
- Vliesofix/Wonderunder
- Fusible batting
- Hobbs Ultra thin batting
- Fabric-marking pen both water and air fading
- Cutting mat, rotary cutter and quilting ruler
- Scissors: dress making, paper, small sharp
- Tape measure and ruler
- Pins
- Hand painted and dyed rayon laces
- Victorian Silk prints
- Wire edge ribbon for making roses and leaves
- Hanah bias ribbons for roses and leaves
- Rayon ribbon for antique roses
- Thread Gatherers ribbon for silk ribbon embroidery
- Hand embroidery, beading and sewing needles

# Victorian Embroidery by Machine

I have always loved hand embroidery, and it was my preferred under-the-desk pastime at school because the clatter of a dropped knitting needle meant instant discovery and a reprimand. Then, as now, if my hands were busy, my mind and body wandered less.

At my mother's knee I discovered the mysteries of grub roses, long and short stitch, blanket stitch, lazy daisy and the many aspects of hand embroidery.

At school I had two remarkable teachers who taught me the meaning of excellence and gave me the will to achieve. These valuable lessons have stayed with me, shaping my approach to machine embroidery.

The 21st century has seen a healthy revival of hand embroidering as well as the production of sewing embroidery machines with creative possibilities never dreamt of. I believed that these machines could so closely replicate hand embroidery that even the most discerning eye could not detect the difference. Using the Pfaff PC-Designer software to digitize embroidery that emulates old fashioned Victorian roses with padded long and short stitching, I took up this challenge. *Victorian Roses* is the result.

## MACHINE EMBROIDERY DESIGNS

Machine embroidery designs come in many forms and can be stored on a pre-programmed memory card, a blank memory card, a floppy disk and a compact disk or on the hard drive of your computer. They can be purchased, personally digitized, downloaded from the Internet or customized to suit your needs.

## PRE-PROGRAMMED MEMORY CARD

These cards, such as the many wonderful Pfaff Fantasy cards with their exquisite designs, are produced by sewing machine companies to suit their own machines. The designs usually come in several sizes and can be combined in the machine memory with other designs when size permits.

## FLOPPY AND COMPACT DISKS

Embroidery designs that come on disks are usually multi-formatted meaning they can be downloaded on to a blank memory card to suit your brand of sewing machine, to be used and stored. This involves PC-Designer software that reads the design disks then, using the software and an interface cable connected to the computer and the machine/card station, transfers the design onto a memory card that can be read by the sewing machine. In some cases a floppy disk can be used directly in the sewing machine.

## PC-DESIGNER SOFTWARE

This software in the hands of an artist is an amazing creative tool. Pfaff was the first domestic sewing machine with design software, introducing it in 1991.

Software allows the user to create personalized designs, alter designs, combine designs, change the size of designs and opens up the world through the Internet so designs can be exchanged and ideas shared.

## MACHINE EMBROIDERY

**A**ll machine embroidery in *Victorian Roses* is **explained in detail in this section and uses the following equipment and materials. The stitch numbers given, the name of the design source and the individual designs will be identified and either stitched from a pre-programmed card or downloaded to a blank memory card via the PC-Designer software.**

- Pfaff Creative 7570 sewing machine
- Pfaff pre-programmed embroidery cards, e.g. Pfaff Roses card No. 36
- Pfaff Creative card – a blank card used to store designs from another source via the PC-Designer software
- Pfaff Choice card – a pre-programmed card that has designs individually chosen by the end user, e.g. Jenny Haskins Choice Card
- Victorian Roses design disk by Jenny Haskins
- Victorian Bows and Baskets design disk by Jenny Haskins
- Victorian Bows and Butterflies, Jenny Haskins signature disk by Cactus Punch
- PC-Designer software, software that interfaces with a sewing machine that allows the end user to digitize designs and transfer these to the sewing machine – used in conjunction with a blank memory card and an interface either with the machine or the Fantasy Card Station
- Size-80/90 embroidery needle
- Pre-wound embroidery bobbins

- Madeira rayon 40 embroidery thread
- Self-adhesive tear-away stabilizer – for motif embroidery
- Water-soluble stabilizer – for lace embroidery
- Photocopy stabilizer – for built-in machine embroidery stitches
- Nylon organza for free-standing embroidery in a color to match

## VICTORIAN ROSES DESIGN DISK

The designs on the Victorian Roses design disk are created so as to replicate hand embroidery as closely as possible. To give the embroiderer as much creative scope as possible we have made the 'bricks' for you to build the 'house' with individual roses, buds, falling roses and leaves so you can create your own personalized designs from those on the design disk. If you are a little less venturesome, we have a rose spray and four wonderful designs in combination with lattice hearts and ovals.

**The roses and leaves are made up of the following:**

—foundation grid to form the basis for the embroidery
—long stitch padding
—the long and short stitching

*LONG STITCH PADDING*

*THE LONG AND SHORT STITCHING*

*THE ROSE IS COMPLETED WITH THE CENTER STAMENS*

The rose is completed with the center stamens. The leaves, falling roses and buds are stitched in a similar fashion. Wonderful machine embroidery is easy, but doesn't just happen, it comes about through practice, knowledge and much perseverance.

The following tips will ensure your success in machine embroidery as you journey through *Victorian Roses*.

### NEEDLES

An embroidery needle has a larger eye than a normal machine needle to allow the thread to pass through the needle without shredding. The thread passing through the needle at speed causes friction, which in turn causes heat resulting in expansion. The larger eye of the needle tolerates the thread expansion and allows the thread to pass easily though the eye of the needle without shredding.

Size 80/90 embroidery needles are recommended.

### THREAD

Most computerized sewing machines work best with a 40-denier thread to give premium results. If the machine you use opens up the stitch density when you enlarge your design, then you may choose to use a slightly thicker 30-denier thread, but only in these cases.

Because of the stitch density, intricate multi-stitch layered lace designs are sometimes best worked with a very fine thread such as a 70/80-denier thread.

I prefer to use Madeira rayon 40 embroidery threads and this is what has been used to achieve the depth of color and sheen in *Victorian Roses*.

### BOBBINS

Who likes to wind bobbins? Not I. With the advent of pre-wound bobbins, machine embroidery is far easier than ever before. Pre-wound embroidery bobbins use a thread denier of 70/80, which is very fine, and thus the bobbin holds more thread than conventional bobbins. Vertical bobbins with a full rotary hook give the best results.

If your machine does not take pre-wound bobbins then use an 80-denier thread in the bobbin or a special thread designed for use in embroidery machine bobbins.

### TENSION

The upper thread tension for machine embroidery is usually between two and three which allows the upper thread to be taken to the underside of the embroidery. You will know when your tension is too loose, as the bobbin thread will show from the top of your embroidery.

To ensure the needle thread is taken to the back of the embroidery, the bobbin tension should be tightened so when the bobbin is held by its thread it won't drop, but will retain its position due to the tighter tension.

*Note: Unsightly loops of needle thread under your embroidery mean that there is no tension on the needle*

*and this usually means that there is thread caught in the upper tension disks, thus holding them open so there is no tension on the upper thread. Avoid this by adhering to the following procedure when changing reels of thread. Always clip your needle thread close to the reel of thread then pull it through the tension disks in the normal direction the thread would pass in the course of sewing. This not only eliminates thread being caught in the tension disks but also helps keep the disks free of lint. The same applies to a bobbin.*

*Threads sitting on rather than in the tension disks will also loop under the embroidery so make sure your thread is secured between the tension disks by releasing the tension every time you change a thread color.*

### STABILIZERS

All machine embroidery needs to be stabilized, that is to say it needs a product that adds body to the fabric being embroidered to hold it flat and smooth so it will not pucker or bunch up with embroidery. There are many stabilizers on the market that do this job well but I will list the ones I use.

#### Self-adhesive tear-away

The self-adhesive tear-away stabilizer is a tear-away stabilizer that has an adhesive side that is covered with a plastic film. This stabilizer is put in an embroidery hoop and allows the embroiderer to place the fabric on the adhesive side of the stabilizer (which is in the hoop) rather than the fabric in the hoop. This not only holds the fabric very taut but also allows for perfect and easy placement of designs.

CUT A PIECE OF SELF-ADHESIVE STABILIZER TO FIT YOUR HOOP

HOOP AND SELF-ADHESIVE STABILIZER, BACKING SIDE UP

REMOVE PROTECTIVE COVERING, SCORING IT WITH A PIN FIRST

POSITION FABRIC ON SELF-ADHESIVE SURFACE AND MACHINE EMBROIDER

PATCH HOLE LEFT BY
EMBROIDERY FROM
UNDERSIDE OF HOOP

## APPLYING EMBROIDERED MOTIFS TO A PROJECT

[A]
TEAR-AWAY STABILIZER
IN HOOP

[B]
ORGANZA PLACED OVER
STICKY SIDE OF STABILIZER

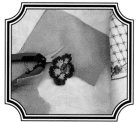

[C]
EMBROIDERY TORN AWAY
FROM STABILIZER AND LEAVES
HOLE IN IT

[D]
CUTTING AWAY ORGANZA
CLOSE TO EMBROIDERY

### Water-soluble stabilizers

These stabilizers dissolve in water, allowing the embroidering of lace designs, which are supported by the stabilizer during the stitching process. When washed, only the embroidery remains. Depending on the type of water-soluble stabilizer you use, the lace may require up to six layers.

## TYPES OF EMBROIDERY

### Direct Embroidery onto the Project

**1. Built-in machine embroidery** using stitches singly, in rows to form one design or combined in a memory to form a completely new stitch or design. Can be altered using PC-Designer software.

**2. Freehand stitching** such as thread painting, stipple-quilting and outline quilting, involves lowering the feed dogs, using a freehand foot and applying a slightly tighter tension in the bobbin and looser upper tension. As the feed dogs are lowered, the artist directs the fabric and it is stitched in a free-wheeling fashion; the fabric is guided by the hand and not advanced by the feed dogs of the machine. Stipple quilting is stitching through three layers of fabric in small meandering and continuous figure eight shapes. Outline quilting is outlining embroidery or an element of a fabric design to quilt and define.

**3. Motif embroidery** requires the fabric to be held taut either in or on a hoop and involves working out the embroidery design combination you wish to sew, using placement marking lines, then placing the fabric over the self-adhesive tear-away stabilizer and embroidering the motifs from the background up. For example if you have roses, leaves and buds, then the buds would be embroidered first, then the leaves over the buds and finally the rose sitting on top of the leaves and buds. You need an embroidery machine, which enables you to stitch with speed and accuracy and is capable of reading embroidery memory cards.

**4. Cut and paste embroidery** is like appliqué. To reduce bulk you embroider a design on a fine fabric then cut the motif out and apply it to another fabric either using a double sided fusible web, glue or by stitching around the outside edge of the design using a transparent thread.

**5. Free standing/three-dimensional embroidery** produces a raised effect on your work and entails embroidering a design such as a leaf or flower on fine fabric, cutting it out and then attaching it to another piece of fabric by the central vein or flower center only.

Having read all the above there is no substitute for practice, practice, practice, so do so before you stitch on the real thing.

Further techniques and tips can be found on pages 94-96 at the back of the book and it is advisable for you to read this also before embarking on the exciting projects in *Victorian Roses*.

# Bags
# &
# Dress Form

## Treasure Bag

❧·❧

*P*erfect for the favorite cameo brooch, grandma's pearls or that special
treasure that needs a home, this little bag is ideal being both practical
and decorative. This project can be done on a basic sewing machine
or should you have an embroidery sewing machine you may wish to replace
the lace cameo with an embroidered Victorian rose or heart.

- 16in (40cm) cream fabric
- 16in (40cm) antiqued 3in (7.5cm) drop edging lace
- 20in (50cm) antiqued ⅜in (1cm) narrow edging lace
- 2 oval 3in (7.5cm) antiqued cameos
- 2 small ribbon roses
- 1 large ribbon rose
- ⅔yd (60cm) variegated silk ribbon 1½in (4cm) wide for tie
- 3in (7.5cm) cream satin ribbon ⅜in (1cm) wide for loops
- Construction thread: cream and antique gold to match the lace
- Universal 75 machine needle
- Normal sewing foot
- General sewing requirements

## PREPARATION

1. Use the template on the pattern sheet to cut four bag pieces from the cream fabric (front and back and two lining pieces.)

2. Use a fabric-marking pen to draw a line ¾in (2cm) from the cut edges around the front of the bag to use as a guide when attaching the narrow edging lace. Also mark the center positions to place the lace cameos on the front and back of the bag.

## ATTACHING THE LACE

3. Use the normal sewing foot and construction thread to match lace to attach the lace cameo in the front and back of the bag, by stitching around the outside edge of the cameo.

4. Stitch the narrow edging lace to the front only of the bag, aligning the straight edge of the lace with the marked line, (scallops to the outside edge of the bag) around the entire front of the bag.

5. Attach the drop lace around the front of the bag with right sides of the lace and fabric together, aligning the straight side of the lace with the raw fabric edge of the front of the bag. Pin the dangling lace ends towards the center of the bag to prevent them being caught in the seams.

6. Cut the cream ribbon in half, then fold each piece in half lengthwise and pin the ends over the lace in the positions marked on either side of the front of the bag – raw edges aligned with the edge of the fabric, loops angled to the center, and stitch in place.

## CONSTRUCTION

7. Place the right sides of the front and back of the bag together then use the cream construction thread to join the front and back of the bag. Join the front and back lining pieces similarly, sewing from the wrong side of the fabric. Trim the seams and clip curves then turn the bag to the right side, remove pins from the drop lace and press both bag and lining.

8. Place the lining bag inside the treasure bag, wrong sides together, aligning all seams. Turn in a hem at the top straight edge on the lining and bag, making sure they align with each other, pin then top stitch ⅛in (4mm) around the edge of the bag catching the lining and the bag together.

9. Use the photo as a guide to color and position of the ribbon rose and either hand sew or glue in place.

10. Thread the variegated ribbon through the ribbon loops at the side of the bag with the ends to the front and tie a bow in the center front to close the treasure bag.

# Victorian Opera Bag

# Victorian Opera Bag

*This Victorian opera bag is the ultimate in style and simplicity proving that it doesn't have to be difficult to look absolutely magnificent and reaffirming the dictum 'work smarter not harder'. Make it from remnants or from a hoarded treasured scrap you never really knew what to do with.*

## MATERIALS

*Note: For machine embroidery materials and techniques refer to pages 10 to 13 before commencing this project.*

- 30in x 9in (75cm x 23cm) strip of striped brocade fabric for the gathered section of the bag
- 30in x 9in (75cm x 23cm) strip of lining fabric
- 10in (25cm) of crushed black velvet fabric for the handle panel
- 1⅛yd (1m) black satin ribbon ⅜in (1cm) wide to thread through casing
- 1⅔yd (1.5m) gold flanged insertion cord to edge handle panel and for the handle
- 10in (25cm) square of medium weight cardboard handle panel
- 10in (25cm) square of medium weight batting for handle panel
- Victorian Roses CD by Jenny Haskins ('openrose' and 'leaf2')
- Construction thread
- Madeira rayon 40 embroidery threads: rose pink 1341, rust rose 1174, light gold 1070, warm brown green 1191, black green 1394 and olive green 1157
- Small pieces of hand-painted lace – two sets of leaves and three small flowers
- Small trinket and ribbon rose
- Bodkin
- Tassel – can be beaded or plain or you may choose to make your own
- Craft glue
- Normal sewing foot
- General sewing requirements

## PREPARATION

**1.** Cut a strip measuring 30in x 9in (75cm x 23cm) from the purse fabric and the lining fabric and pin them, wrong sides together, around all raw fabric edges.

**2.** Use the handle panel template on the pattern sheet to cut four cardboard and two batting half ovals, omitting the seam allowance, for the center front and back and lining of the purse. Use the craft glue to attach the batting to the right side of the front and back cardboard pieces only.

**3.** Use the same template but with seam allowance added to cut from the crushed velvet the center front and back and lining pieces of the purse. Draw around the template then cut out the crushed velvet fabric. Cut four, one each for the front and back and two for the lining.

**4.** Refer to diagram No 1 on the pattern sheet to measure down on either side of the long edge of the purse fabric and lining 1¾in (4.5cm) and make a cut the width of the seam allowance.

**5.** Press the 1¾in (4.5cm) seam allowances to the lining side of the purse fabric strip and press.

## EMBROIDERY

**6.** Use the photo as a guide to color and position to embroider 'leaf2' then position 'openrose' over the leaves in the center front crushed velvet oval of the purse.

## CONSTRUCTION

**7.** Center the front and back crushed velvet over the batting side of the cardboard with the wrong side of velvet to right side of batting. Place a pin in the center to hold the velvet in place. Run glue around the back of the cardboard then pull the velvet to the back of the cardboard and glue down making sure the front is tight and the velvet is flat and even. Repeat for the lining sections of the front and back of the purse.

**8.** Cut the gold flanged insertion cord in half then glue the flange to the back of the cardboard on the center front and back velvet panels starting and finishing at the center front. Unravel each end of the cord then twist the ends together to form a continuous cord, with the raw ends to the back of the work and make sure they are firmly secured with the glue.

9. Cut the flange from the cord that rises above the black velvet to form the cord-only handles. (See diagram on pattern sheet.)

10. Glue the tassel to the center front of the velvet panel, so the tassel hangs down.

11. To make the casing at either end of the purse fabric and lining, fold under a narrow ¼in (6mm) hem to the lining side of the fabric strip then a ½in (12mm) hem and then stitch down using matching construction thread and a normal sewing foot.

12. Gather up either long side of the purse and lining fabric so it exactly fits around the curved edge of the center front and back velvet panels.

13. Glue to the wrong side of each curved edge of the handle panels making sure to start and finish on either side just below the casing.

14. Glue the velvet lining panels to the front and back panels making sure the edges exactly align and that all raw fabric edges are covered and that the tassel sits over the front of the purse.

15. Cut the narrow satin ribbon in half, then use the bodkin to thread it through the casing on either side of the purse. Pull up the ribbon to complete the purse and finish with a bow on either side.

16. Use the photo as a guide to position then glue the lace leaves and flowers, the trinket and the ribbon rose to the center front of the purse.

## Decorative Dress Form

*T*his miniature Victorian dress form will enhance any sewing room, bringing charm to a special corner. It is also useful for displaying Victorian pins, brooches or earrings which in turn add to the appeal of the dress form.

*Note: Decorating the dress form is very easy and for a first attempt it is very costly to purchase a purpose-made stand and top. Why not use a candleholder or a discarded lamp base for the stand and find a curtain rod end or teapot lid to give an inexpensive finishing touch.*

### MATERIALS

*Note: For requirements and machine embroidery techniques refer to pages 12 and 13 before commencing this project.*

- 1 small papier maché dress form (available from most craft stores)
- 15in (38cm) tubular ribbing in the color of your choice
- 18in (46cm) bead fringing 6in (15cm) wide
- 26in (66cm) chenille and silk ribbon edging braid ¾in (2cm) wide
- 1 large triangular lace medallion
- 1 antique button or discarded earring
- 1in (2.5cm) antique bead fringing
- 2 crystal beads
- 1 dragonfly trinket
- Victorian Roses CD by Jenny Haskins
- Madeira rayon 40 embroidery thread: dark burgundy 1385, rose pink 1054, pale rose pink 1142, yellow gold 1070, rose gold 1026, olive green 1057 and black green 1394
- Craft glue
- Sharp knife
- General sewing requirements

### PREPARATION

1. Cut a small hole in the center of the top and bottom of the dress form using the sharp knife.

2. Place the tubular ribbing over the papier maché dress form making sure it fits snugly to the dress form. If necessary make a center back seam to ensure the correct fit.

3. Use a pointed object to push the excess ribbing through the holes at the top and bottom of the dress form, securing the fabric with glue.

4. If your stand and the top for the stand need painting or staining, do so before assembly. Support the dress form on the stand and top with your chosen piece then glue both in place.

### DECORATING THE DRESS FORM

5. Glue the beaded fringe to the bottom of the dress form then the braid over the top of the ribbon header.

**6.** Glue the 1in (2.5cm) antique beaded fringe center front of the neck, then glue the chenille edging around the neck, starting and finishing at the center front over the beads. Glue a button over the join.

**7.** Glue the triangular lace motif over the shoulders of the dress form so it becomes a shawl, gluing only the inside edge of the lace so the remainder falls free.

---

### EMBROIDERY

**8.** Use the threads from the materials list to embroider three 'openrose', one leaf1 and one leaf2, from Victorian Roses CD by Jenny Haskins, using the freestanding technique.

**9.** Use the photo as a guide to color and position and glue the leaves under the three roses on the bottom right hand side of the dress form.

**10.** Use the photo as a guide to position then glue the dragonfly and the two crystal beads.

## *Victorian Purse Necklace*

*H*ow inventive, opulent and totally marvelous to have an exquisite necklace that is a purse also. It is ideal for keeping business cards, sewing essentials, small bottles of perfume or any items you need close at hand when a large purse is not necessary.

- 6in (15cm) moiré taffeta
- 1 Victorian Small 1053 print by Jenny Haskins on moiré taffeta
- 6in (15cm) light weight fusible batting
- 5in (13cm) beaded fringe 6in (15cm) long for bottom of purse
- 20in (50cm) antiqued 1in (25mm) edging lace for around the outside front of the heart
- 1⅛yd (1m) antiqued ½in (12mm) edging lace for around the inside front and back of the heart
- 16in (40cm) Victorian silk ribbon flower trim
- Antique seed beads in black luster, beading needle and thread
- 1 small butterfly trinket
- Madeira black rayon 40 embroidery thread for twisted cord for around the neck and cream thread for construction and freehand quilting
- Hand sewing needle
- Machine feet: normal sewing foot and clear-view freehand foot
- Size-80 embroidery needle
- 1 empty bobbin
- Craft glue
- General sewing requirements

## PREPARATION

1. Use the heart template from the pattern sheet and the fabric-marking pen to trace around then cut out three hearts from the moiré taffeta and four from the lightweight fusible batting.

2. Use the above template centered over the heart-print and trace around it.

3. Iron the fusible batting to the back of the four moiré hearts.

## QUILTING

4. Use the clear-view freehand foot, size-80 needle and the cream rayon embroidery thread to outline quilt the rose motif in the center of the print then stipple quilt the background fabric.

## BEADING

5. Use the seed beads, beading needle and thread to bead the center of the heart print with a bead on each intersecting line.

6. Retrace the heart shape on the center front of the purse to allow for shrinkage due to quilting then cut out the purse front.

7. Stitch the antique 1in (2.5cm) edging lace to the outside edge of the beaded purse front. Right sides of lace and fabric together, straight edge of lace and fabric aligned, stitching from the wrong side of the lace.

8. Place the right side of the beaded purse front to the right side of one purse lining and stitch together from the wrong side of the fabric around the outside edge of the heart allowing a ¼in (6mm) seam. Leave a 3in (7.5cm) opening on one side for turning. Repeat for the back of the heart.

9. Turn both front and back heart pieces to the right side and press. Turn the opening seam allowance on the turning opening to the wrong side of the fabric, press then pin.

10. Top stitch around the hearts, close to the fabric edge, while stitching the turning opening closed.

11. Stitch the ½in (12mm) edging lace to the inside edge of the purse front and back aligning the straight edge of the lace with the top stitching and with the scalloped edge of the lace to the center of the heart.

12. Double up the ribbon edge of the beaded fringe, then pin and stitch this around the center front, on the lining side, of the bottom of the heart.

13. Center the front of the purse over the back with the lining sides together, making sure all sides align then stitch around the outside edge of the hearts, leaving a 3in (7.5cm) opening at the top of the purse.

14. Refer to page 97 for the twisted cord technique, then attach this cord on either side of the opening at the top of the heart using a hand-sewing needle. Choose a length that is suitable to your needs.

15. Use the beading needle and thread and seed beads to hand bead the inside edging lace.

16. Use the craft glue to glue the silk ribbon trim around the outside edge of the front of the purse then use the photo as guide to position then glue the butterfly trinket to the bottom of the heart print on the front of the purse.

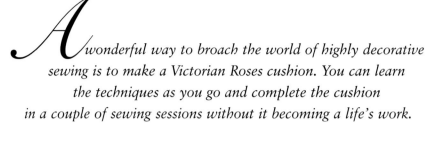

*A wonderful way to broach the world of highly decorative sewing is to make a Victorian Roses cushion. You can learn the techniques as you go and complete the cushion in a couple of sewing sessions without it becoming a life's work.*

## Beaded Cushion

Finished size of cushion 21in (53cm).

### MATERIALS

- 18in (46cm) grey-green silk dupion (fabric is pin tucked to form a diagonal grid then a seed pearl is stitched over each intersecting pin tuck)
- 24in (61cm) floral border and backing fabric
- 24in (61cm) fusible batting to back cushion front
- 1¾yd (1.5m) piping cord
- 2⅔yd (2.45m) beaded lace 3in (7.5cm) wide
- 3 hand-painted lace motifs
- Victorian lady print by Jenny Haskins No 1077
- 10in (25cm) Vliesofix/Wonderunder
- Madeira rayon 40 gray green embroidery thread
- Construction thread
- Monofilament thread
- Pre-wound embroidery bobbin
- Size-80 embroidery needle
- Machine feet: open-toe foot, zipper foot, clear-view freehand foot and normal sewing foot
- Hand sewing needle
- 14in (36cm) cushion insert
- General sewing requirements

### PREPARATION

**1. FROM THE PIN TUCKED FABRIC CUT:**

—one, 16in (41cm) square for the cushion front
—one, 2in (5cm) strip across the width of the fabric with a row of pearls centered for piping

**FROM THE FLORAL FABRIC CUT:**

—two 3½in (9cm) strips across the width of the fabric for border of the cushion top
—one 22in (56cm) square for the cushion back

**FROM THE FUSIBLE BATTING CUT:**

—one, 16in (41cm) square to back the cushion front

—two, 3½in (9cm) strips across the width of batting for the cushion borders
—one, 7in x 10in (18cm x 25cm) rectangle to back the print

**2.** Iron the Vliesofix/Wonderunder to the back of colored lace motifs. (See page 94 to apply fusible web to the back of lace.)

**3.** Trim the fabric around the silk print to measure 7in x 10in (18cm x 25cm) then iron the batting rectangle to the back of the silk print.

**4.** Iron Vliesofix/Wonderunder to the back of the above batting on the back of the print.

**5.** Center the print on the silk dupion and draw around it with a fabric-marking pen. Remove the pearls from inside this area.

**6.** Iron the print to the center front of the cushion.

**7.** Iron the fusible batting square to the underside of the cushion top and the border fabric.

**8.** Cut the border fabric into two 16in (41cm) strips for the top and bottom of the cushion and two 22in (56cm) strips for the sides.

**9.** Cut the lace motifs into suitably sized pieces to frame the print and put to one side.

### THE PRINT

**10.** Use the open-toe foot, size-80 embroidery needle, gray green thread in the needle, pre-wound bobbin and stitch No 16 width 1.5, length 0.7 to stitch around the outside edge of the print fabric and the edge of the print.

**11.** Arrange the cut lace motif pieces around the print using the photo as a guide to position, then iron in place using a hot steam iron.

**12.** Use the clear-view freehand foot, monofilament thread and a freehand straight stitch to attach the lace motifs following the outside edge of each motif.

*TOP LEFT: JENNY HASKINS ROSE PRINTS WERE TRIMMED AT THE CORNERS AND SATIN STITCHED WITH GOLD METALLIC THREAD AND THIS STITCHING WAS EDGED WITH A TRIPLE STITCH TO GIVE A DEEPLY TOP STITCHED EFFECT. THE BROCADE TRIMMED CUSHION CONSTRUCTION IS THE SAME AS FOR THE BEADED CUSHION.*

# Romantic Cushions

### PIPING

**13.** Fold the piping strip of fabric in half lengthwise, wrong sides together, over the piping cord, so the row of pearls sits exactly on the fold. Use the zipper foot and needle positions to stitch close to the piping cord.

**14.** Attach the piping to the outside edge of the cushion front, right sides of fabric together, raw edges aligned, stitching with the underside of the piping uppermost, using the zipper foot and needle positions to stitch close to the edge of the piping.

### BORDERS

**15.** Attach the 16in (41cm) border fabric strips to the top and bottom of the cushion, right sides of fabric together stitching from the wrong side of the border fabric. Attach the 22in (56cm) side border strips in a similar way.

### PUTTING IT TOGETHER

**16.** Pin the cushion backing to the cushion top, right sides together, raw edges aligned. (Cushion backing is the same size as the cushion front plus its borders.)

**17.** Stitch around all sides, leaving an 8in (20cm) opening for turning.

**18.** Turn the cushion to the right side and press the seams. Pin the cushion top to the cushion backing on the outside edge of the piping then use the zipper foot to stitch around the piping leaving an opening to match the opening at the edge of the border.

**19.** Place the cushion insert in the center of the cushion, pin the piping opening to close it then stitch the opening closed close to the outside edge of the piping.

**20.** Turn the seam allowance in to the wrong side on the border opening, pin then top stitch around the edge of the border fabric closing the turning opening.

**21.** Use the hand sewing needle and matching thread to lace to hand sew the beaded lace over the border fabric, the straight side of the lace sitting under the piping, wrong side of lace to right side of border fabric.

Miter each corner (see page 95 to miter a corner.)

## *Bolster*

*A* bolster cushion always adds a finishing touch to pillows at the top of a bed, perfect for that love seat or just scattered on your favorite couch. This bolster cushion is functional, decorative and very easy to make on a basic sewing machine.

### MATERIALS

- 24in (60cm) brocade fabric
- 24in (60cm) fusible batting
- 8in (20cm) pale pink silk dupion for frill
- 1 Victorian Rose print by Jenny Haskins No 1053
- 12in (30cm) Vliesofix/Wonderunder
- 1½yd (1.4m) medium piping cord
- 2 green bolster end tassels
- 4in (10cm) black lace suitable for cutting to form a circle
- 1 packet green antique seed beads
- Beading needle and thread
- Hand sewing needle
- Machine feet: normal sewing foot, open-toe foot, clear-view freehand foot and zipper foot
- Machine needle: size-80 embroidery needle
- Madeira rayon 40 gray green embroidery thread
- Monofilament thread
- Construction thread
- Toyfil
- General sewing requirements

### PREPARATION

**1.** FROM THE BROCADE FABRIC CUT:

—one, 18in x 22in (45cm x 55cm) rectangle for the bolster front

—two, 4in x 22in (10cm x 55cm) rectangles for each end

—one, 2in (5cm) bias strip joined to measure 48in (1.2m) for piping

**FROM THE PINK SILK DUPION CUT:**

—two, 8in (20cm) strips across the width of the fabric for the frills

**FROM THE FUSIBLE BATTING CUT:**

—one, 18in x 22in (45cm x 55cm) rectangle to back the brocade rectangle

—one, 10in (25cm) square for the back of the print

**2.** Iron the Vliesofix/Wonderunder to the back of the black lace and cut out lace motifs to cover the edge of the Victorian print.

**3.** Iron the corresponding fusible batting pieces to the backs of the brocade fabric rectangle and the Victorian print.

## QUILTING

**4.** Use the open-toe foot, size-80 embroidery needle, grey green rayon thread and a straight stitch to quilt the diagonal grid in the center of the heart.

**5.** Use the clear-view freehand foot and a freehand straight-stitch to outline-quilt the flowers and leaves of the print using monofilament thread.

## BEADING

**6.** Use the antique seed beads, the beading needle and thread to stitch four beads at each intersection of the lines of the diagonal grid on the heart print.

## CONSTRUCTION

**7.** Cut around the beaded print, ¾in (2cm) from the edge of the heart and the roses.

**7.** Center the beaded print on the front of the brocade fabric backed with batting. Pin the print in place then use the monofilament thread, a narrow zig-zag and the open-toe foot to stitch around the raw edges of the fabric print.

**8.** Place the black lace motifs around the print to form a circle with a diameter of 10in (25cm), pin then iron in place using a hot steam iron.

**9.** Use the clear-view freehand foot, a freehand straight stitch and monofilament thread to stitch around the outside and inside edge of the lace circle following the outline of the lace.

**10.** Fold the 2in (5cm) strip of brocade fabric in half lengthwise, wrong sides together, enfolding the piping

cord. Use the zipper foot and needle positions to stitch the piping strip close to the edge of the cord.

**11.** Cut piping into two equal lengths.

**12.** Fold the pink silk dupion frill strips in half lengthwise and gather up to fit the 21½in (55cm) edges of the brocade rectangle. Start and finish the gathering stitching on the folded edge of the frill. This will pull the raw fabric ends of the frill into the seam allowance so there is no joining seam in the frill and no raw fabric edges will show.

**13.** Use the zipper foot to attach the piping to each 21½in (55cm) edge of the brocade fabric with right side of piping and brocade fabric together, raw fabric edges aligned stitching from the wrong side of the piping, close to the edge of the cord. Attach the frill over the piping, right sides of frill to wrong side of piping, raw edges of piping and frill aligned, stitching on the wrong side of the frill. Start and finish the frill ¼in (6mm) from the edge of the center back seam.

**14.** Attach the 4in x 22in (10cm x 55cm) brocade rectangles over the frill, right side of brocade fabric to wrong side of frill, raw edges aligned, stitching from the wrong side of the brocade rectangle.

**15.** Fold the bolster in half lengthwise, right sides together, and seam down the wrong side of the fabric keeping the frill clear of this seam.

**16.** Gather up one end of the bolster, pulling the fabric into a gathered circle using a hand sewing needle and beading thread and secure. Position the bolster end tassel over the gathered up end and hand stitch in place to cover the gathering.

**17.** Insert the Toyfil in the bolster, filling out the cylindrical shape of the cushion. (The gathered end should sit flat.)

**18.** Complete the bolster by gathering up the open end to match the other end, completing with a bolster end tassel.

*Victorian*
*Tea Party*

# Milk Jug Cover

*In Victorian times milk was kept in gauzed pantries which usually were in the
coldest part of the house or even external to the house.
In the early part of the 20th century the ice chest was introduced to keep
food cold. Milk which was usually kept in a jug or bucket was covered
with a net cover to keep insects at bay; this developed into a decorative
beaded net cover that graced many a dainty jug at a Victorian tea party.
Today it is mainly decorative,
but still has a practical use.*

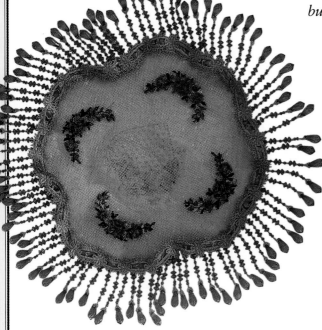

## MATERIALS

*Note: For machine embroidery materials and
techniques refer to pages 10 to 13 before commencing
this project.*

- ❧ 10in (25cm) square of antique cotton netting
- ❧ 30in (75cm) antiqued double edged lace beading ¾in (2cm) wide
- ❧ 30in (75cm) beaded fringe 3in (7.5cm) wide
- ❧ Pfaff Roses card No 36
- ❧ Madeira rayon 40 embroidery threads: rose pink 1054, dark rose pink 1341 gray green 1306, and black green 1493
- ❧ Construction thread to match the antique lace
- ❧ Normal sewing foot
- ❧ General sewing requirements

## PREPARATION

**1.** Cut the net into a 10in (25cm) square then fold it
through the center twice and then across the
diagonal. Measure 4½in (11.5cm) from the folded
point and scribe an arc from side to side marking
with pins or a pen. Connect the marks and cut along
the marked line. When opened out, it will be a circle.

**2.** Prior to opening the net, measure 1in (2.5cm)
from each end of the arc along the straight lines.
Determine the center point of the arc. Join these
three points in another arc to make a scallop.
Cut along this line, open up the net and there will be
eight even scallops around the edge of the circular
piece of net.

## EMBROIDERY

**3.** Use the photo as guide to position and color to
embroider four design No 18 from Pfaff Roses card
No 36 equally spaced around the net cover, that are
3in (7.5cm) from the center of the circle.

## EDGE

**4.** Stitch the ribbon header from the beaded fringe
under the insertion lace to represent ribbon threaded
through the lace.

**5.** Attach the lace with the attached beading around
the edge of the net, following the scalloped edge,
using the normal sewing foot and construction thread
that matches the color of the lace.

*Note: The milk jug cover has a Victorian
print centered in it, these are available from Jenny
Haskins Designs as a special order. If you do not have
an embroidery machine, appliqué or lace motifs can
replace the embroidery.*

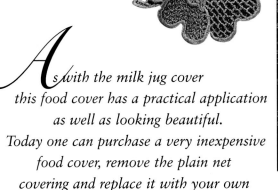

*As with the milk jug cover
this food cover has a practical application
as well as looking beautiful.
Today one can purchase a very inexpensive
food cover, remove the plain net
covering and replace it with your own
decorative cover, using the original net as a pattern for the new cover.*

## Food Cover

### MATERIALS

- Purchased net-covered food protector
- 15in (38cm) antique cotton netting (a Victorian rose print is centered in each panel after the net is cut out)
- 2yd (2m) antiqued drop lace 3in (7.5cm) wide
- 20in (50cm) wire edged ribbon 1½in (4cm) wide
- 5 pink ribbon roses
- 1 tassel
- 20in (50cm) gold cord
- Normal machine sewing foot and needle
- Craft glue
- General sewing requirements

### PREPARATION

1. Un-pick the net cover from the purchased food cover and use it as a template to cut four net segments for the food cover. (Net prints are available from Jenny Haskins Designs.)

### CONSTRUCTION

2. Join the four segments together using construction thread and a normal sewing foot and needle.

3. Attach the drop lace to the top and bottom of the joined net segments with wrong side of lace to right side of net and the drops falling to the bottom of the cover (use the photo as a guide).

4. Join the last segment of the cover. Trim all seams and press flat.

### PUTTING IT TOGETHER

5. Replace the pull up cord with the gold cord and attach a tassel to the end that pulls up the food cover.

6. Fully extend the food cover (make sure the top is clicked into place).

7. Place the net cover over the wire struts, aligning seams with struts, and make sure the net fits tightly around the top and bottom of the cover. You may need to ease and adjust some of the seams.

8. Use the glue to attach the bottom seam of segments to the plastic tips at the bottom of each strut. Glue a rose on the right side of the lace and net to cover each of these plastic tips.

9. Use the ribbon to gather up the top of the cover and tie securely finishing with a bow with a ribbon rose in the center.

# Tablecloth

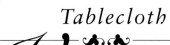

*V*ictorian ladies
were known for their exquisite hand
embroidery, whiling away their many leisure
hours. Today these hours
are in short supply yet we still love the hand
embroidered look of the Victorian era.
Victorian Roses embroidery CD is my dream
come true. In conjunction with the Pfaff
embroidery machine, hand embroidery can
be exactly replicated to such a level that it
defies detection, even from the most fervent
hand embroiderers.

*Note: I have used an antique tablecloth
from my private collection then embroidered
the center of it around an inserted oval doily. You
may choose to do the same or make your tablecloth
from scratch – from the materials list.*

**Finished size of tablecloth 53in (135cm) square**

## MATERIALS

*Note: For machine embroidery materials and
techniques refer to pages 10 to 13 before commencing
this project.*

- 56in (142cm) square of table linen
- 7⅓yd (7.40m) hand made edging lace
  3½in (9cm) wide
- 1 antique oval doily 10in x 17in (25cm x 43cm)
- Victorian Roses CD by Jenny Haskins
- Machine feet: open-toe embroidery foot
- Machine needles: size-80
  embroidery needle and
  120-wing needle
- Construction thread, cream

- Madeira rayon 40 embroidery threads: rust rose
  1174, deep burgundy 1385, yellow gold 1070,
  rose gold 1126, antique gold 1338, grey green
  1306, olive green 1157, warm-brown green 1191
  and black green 1393
- Fray stopper
- Duck-billed scissors
- General sewing requirements

## PREPARATION

**1.** Cut table linen to a 56in (142cm) square.

**2.** Fold under a double hem around the tablecloth
and press, pin at intervals if necessary.

**3.** Center the oval doily in the linen square and pin
around the edges so both the doily and linen are flat
and smooth.

**4.** Use the fabric-marking pen to draw an oval
around the doily that is 2in (5cm) from the edge of
the doily. Extend the oval with 'twig' lines at intervals
on either side of the line to position leaves.

## HEM STITCHING

**5.** Use the 120-wing needle, cream construction
thread in the needle and bobbin and the open-toe
foot to attach the hem around the edge of the linen
tablecloth using stitch No 112 length normal and
width 2.5. Stitch from the right side of the fabric
making sure the hole is punched in the single layer
of fabric and the needle swings over the folded edge
of the hem (at the back of the cloth) to catch it down
while creating a hemstitched edge. Continue across
each corner to the folded edge of the hem.

**6.** Attach the wide antique edging lace to the folded
edge of the hem on the right side of the fabric. The
straight edge of the lace just sits over the folded hem
edge of the tablecloth and the scalloped edge faces
out. Attach the lace using cream construction thread,
open toe foot and a narrow zigzag stitch, mitering
each corner as you sew. Refer to page 95 for a
mitered corner.

## CENTER DOILY

**7.** Attach the doily to the center of the linen using a
double row of straight stitching, using the open-toe
foot and matching thread in the needle and bobbin
following the shape of the doily.

**11.** Use the positioning template on the pattern sheet to mark the position and colors of each embroidered rose, leaf, bud and falling rose.

**12.** Use the open-toe foot, antique gold rayon thread and stitch No 16 width 1.5 length 0.7 to stitch the penciled oval and 'twigs' around the doily in the center of the tablecloth.

**13.** Embroider the rose garland following the numbered sequence and the thread colors used from the pattern sheet. Use the photo as a guide also.

*Note: This type of replicated hand embroidery is very stitch intense and thus time consuming so be patient – the end result is worth the wait. Remember that to embroider this by hand would take many hundreds of hours.*

*TIP: Clip the jump threads as you go, as this improves the quality of the finished embroidery.*

**8.** You may choose to leave the linen fabric under a section of the doily. If so, stitch on either side of this section to secure it.

**9.** If not, use a small sharp pair of duck-billed scissors to cut the linen from under the doily. To prevent fraying you may need to apply fray stopper to the edges of the linen.

**10.** Press doily when the above is completed.

## Place-mat

### ❧❧

*T*he place-mat, tea cozy, table runner
*and serviette are all made with matching
fabric to form a Victorian set.*

*Note: These four projects require 1½yd (1.5m)
of brocade and cream fabric. Fabric measurements will
be given for the individual projects.*

### MATERIALS

*Note: For machine embroidery materials
and techniques refer to pages 10 to 13 before
commencing this project.*

- 14in x 11in (36cm x 28cm) rectangle of brocade
  fabric

- 3in (7.5cm) strip of brocade fabric on the bias
  joined together to measure 56in (142cm) for the
  edge of the place-mat

- 14in x 11in (36cm x 28cm) fusible batting to
  back the above

- 15in x 11in (38cm x 28cm) cream fabric for
  backing

- 7in (18cm) square cream fabric for bottom corner
  of place-mat

- 7in (18cm) square of fusible batting to back the above

- 1yd 23in (150cm) antiqued edging lace 2in (5cm)
  wide

- 50in (130cm) gold insertion cord

- 12in (30cm) olive green frilled silk ribbon 1½in
  (4cm) wide

- Victorian Roses CD by Jenny Haskins

- Small pieces of nylon organza in the colors
  of the roses

- Madeira rayon 40 embroidery thread: rust rose
  1174, dark burgundy 1385, apricot 1053, dusky
  rose 1054, dark rose 1341, warm-brown green
  1191 and olive green 1157

- Construction thread

- Monofilament thread

- Machine feet: open-toe foot, zipper
  foot and clear-view freehand foot

- Hand sewing needle

- General sewing
  requirements

## PREPARATION

**1. USE THE MEASUREMENTS
IN THE MATERIALS LIST TO CUT:**

—from the brocade the front of the place-mat and the binding
—from the fusible batting the brocade backing
—from the cream fabric the place-mat backing
—the cream square in half on the diagonal

**2. IRON THE FUSIBLE BATTING TO:**

—the back of the brocade rectangle for the front of the place-mat
—the back of the cream triangle for the corner of the place-mat.

**3.** On one corner of the brocade backed with fusible batting, measure 6in (15cm) from either side of the corner then fold the corner to the wrong side on the diagonal and pin. Cut the folded edge to allow a ¾in (2cm) seam-allowance.

**4.** Join the bias strips to measure 56cm (142cm), then fold it in half lengthwise and press. Turn under and press a ¾in (2cm) hem allowance on one long edge of the bias strip.

## EMBROIDERY

**5.** Use the organza and the freestanding technique to embroider two 'openrose' and one 'rose2' (flower only) using the photo as a guide to colors used. When embroidery is complete cut the three flowers out close to the edge of the stitching.

**6.** Use the green threads to embroider three sets of 'leaf1'on the cream triangular fabric, two sets along the diagonal edge and one set in the corner with a gap in the middle for the freestanding roses.

## PUTTING IT ALL TOGETHER

**7.** Place the cream embroidered triangle under the folded brocade corner of the place-mat, right side of cream fabric to underside of brocade fabric so the embroidered leaves appear to be coming from under the brocade fabric, and pin. Use the open-toe foot and matching thread to stitch the above together from the right side of the brocade, ¾in (2cm) from the folded diagonal edge.

**8.** Fold the olive-green frilled ribbon in half length-wise and attach it over the diagonal corner seam on the right side of the brocade fabric with the fold parallel to the brocade fold, stitching along the edge of the frill using matching green thread to ribbon.

## QUILTING

**9.** Pin the cream backing fabric to the underside of the place mat then use matching cream thread in the bobbin and needle and the clear-view freehand foot to stipple-quilt around the embroidered leaves on the corner cream fabric.

**10.** Use monofilament thread in the needle to outline quilt the rose designs on the brocade fabric on the front of the place-mat.

## FINISHING OFF

**11.** Trim the place-mat to the correct size and round the corners then use the zipper foot and needle positions to attach the insertion cord around the outside edge of the quilted fabric. Align the edge of the flange with the raw fabric edge, wrong side of flange to right side of fabric, stitching from the right side, clipping the corners as you sew. Overlap the cord to join.

**12.** Attach the binding to the edge of the place-mat, right sides of binding to right side of the place mat, raw fabric edges of mat and binding aligned, fold to the center and stitch close to the edge of the cord using the zipper foot and needle positions.

**13.** Leave 2in (5cm) on either end then join the binding on the bias to complete the outside edge of the mat.

**14.** Fold the binding over to the back of the mat, pin, then use the zipper foot to stitch-in-the-ditch from the right side of the mat, close to the edge of the cord to catch the binding down on its fold at the back of the mat.

**15.** Using the photo as a guide to position and the hand-sewing needle and thread, stitch the freestanding roses in place in the corner of the mat.

**16.** Use the hand sewing needle and thread to attach the antique edging lace around the outside edge at the back of the mat — right side of lace to right side of backing fabric, with the scallops facing out.

# Tea Cozy

*Note: For machine embroidery materials and techniques refer to pages 10 to 13 before commencing this project.*

- 14in x 20in (36cm x 50cm) brocade fabric
- 14cm x 32in (36cm x 60cm) cream fabric
- 14in x 1yd (36cm x 1m) fusible batting
- 30in (76cm) flanged insertion cord
- 26in (66cm) olive green frilled edge silk ribbon 1½in (4cm) wide
- 26in (66cm) antique edging lace 2in (5cm) wide
- 1 tassel

- Victorian Roses CD by Jenny Haskins
- Pink/red nylon organza for freestanding embroidery
- Madeira rayon 40 embroidery thread: rust rose 1174, dark burgundy 1385, apricot 1053, dusky rose 1054, dark rose 1341, warm-brown green 1191 and olive green 1157
- Construction thread
- Monofilament thread
- Machine feet: open-toe foot, zipper foot and clear-view freehand foot
- Hand sewing needle
- General sewing requirements

## PREPARATION

1. USE THE TEMPLATE ON THE PATTERN SHEET TO CUT:
—two from the brocade
—four from the fusible batting
—two from the cream lining fabric.

2. Iron the fusible batting to the above fabric pieces.

3. From the cream lining fabric and fusible batting cut two rectangles 8in x 13in (20cm x 33cm).

## EMBROIDERY

4. On one piece of the cream lining rectangle starting 1in (2.5cm) from one long straight edge use the green threads to embroider three sets of 'leaf1' from the Victorian Roses CD. Evenly space the leaves rotating them so they face in different directions.

5. Use the photo as a guide to thread colors used from the materials list to embroider three 'openrose' and two 'rose2' (one mirrored) using the freestanding technique. When embroidery is complete cut around the edge of each rose close to the stitching.

## QUILTING

6. Iron the fusible batting to the back of the cream fabric rectangles. Use the clear-view freehand foot and cream thread to stipple-quilt both the back and embroidered front cream rectangles.

7. Use the monofilament thread to outline-quilt the back and front brocade half circles of the tea cozy.

## PUTTING IT TOGETHER

8. Fold the straight side of the brocade fabric to the back of the front and back of the tea cozy, using the guideline on the template from the pattern sheet.

9. Place the cream embroidered rectangle under the folded brocade on the straight edge of the tea cozy, right side of cream fabric to underside of folded brocade fabric so the embroidered leaves appear to be coming from under the brocade fabric, and pin. Use the open-toe foot and matching thread to stitch the above together from the right side of the brocade,

1in (2.5cm) from the folded straight edge.

10. Use matching thread to the ribbon to stitch it across the hemline at the bottom of the tea cozy on the brocade. Stitch top and bottom of ribbon under the frill.

11. Repeat steps 8 and 9 for the back.

12. Use the zipper foot and needle positions to attach the flanged insertion cord around the front of the tea cozy, right sides of flange and brocade together with the straight edge of the flange aligned with the fabric edge of the front of tea cozy. Start and finish 3in (7.5cm) under the folded brocade on the cream fabric on either side of the tea cozy.

13. Use the open-toe foot to stitch the cream lining half circle to the bottom edge of the quilted cream fabric on the back and front tea cozy pieces – right sides together stitching from the wrong side.

14. Top stitch the seam on the lining side of the half circle.

15. Place the front and back together (with the lining attached) right sides together, edges aligned and the end of the insertion cord to the outside fabric edge, and pin.

16. Stitch around the outside edge of the tea cozy and lining, using the zipper foot leaving a 6in (15cm) turning opening on the curved edge of the tea cozy lining. Trim all seams and clip curved edges.

17. Turn under the seam allowance on the turning opening and pin then top stitch close to the edge of the fabric to secure the opening closed.

18. Top stitch around the front of the tea cozy, ¼in (6mm) from the edge, starting and stopping with the insertion cord.

19. Use the hand-sewing needle and thread to attach the tassel to the center top of the front of the cozy. Push the lining inside the tea cozy until the bottom fold aligns with insertion cord.

20. Hand sew the antique edging lace ½in (12mm) up from the bottom folded edge of the tea cozy and lining so the scalloped edge of the lace drops below the fold. Use the photo as a guide to color and position of the embroidered roses. Pin then hand sew them in place making sure some roses overlap the folded brocade and the edging lace.

# Napkin

*Note: For machine embroidery materials and techniques refer to pages 10 to 13 before commencing this project.*

## MATERIALS

- 16in (40cm) square of cream fabric
- 1¾in (4cm) brocade bias strip joined together to measure 1¾yd (1.6m)
- Victorian Roses CD by Jenny Haskins design 'rose2'
- Rayon 40 embroidery thread: rose pink 1054, dark rose 1341, olive green 1157 and black green 1393
- Open-toe machine foot
- General sewing requirements

## PREPARATION

**1.** Cut the cream fabric square and the brocade bias strip.

**2.** Fold the bias strip in half lengthwise and press.

## EMBROIDERY

**3.** Use the thread in the materials list to embroider 'rose2' centered in one corner of the cream fabric square.

## PUTTING IT TOGETHER

**4.** Place the brocade bias binding around the edge of the napkin, right sides of bias to right side of napkin, raw fabric edges aligned stitching from the wrong side of the bias using cream construction thread and the open-toe foot. Round the corners and join the binding in the same manner as the place mat. Trim the seam and clip the corners.

**5.** Press and pin the binding to the back of the napkin then stitch-in-the-ditch from the right side of the napkin to attach the binding to the back of the napkin.

# Table Runner

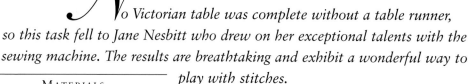

*No Victorian table was complete without a table runner, so this task fell to Jane Nesbitt who drew on her exceptional talents with the sewing machine. The results are breathtaking and exhibit a wonderful way to play with stitches.*

## MATERIALS

- ❧ 13in (33cm) brocade fabric for top of runner
- ❧ 24in (61cm) cream fabric for backing and center of runner
- ❧ 13in (33cm) fusible batting
- ❧ 12in (30cm) Vliesofix/Wonderunder
- ❧ 1 Victorian print, large rose print No 1051 by Jenny Haskins
- ❧ 4 corner antiqued lace motifs
- ❧ 24in (61cm) antiqued 12in (30cm) fringe for tassels
- ❧ Pfaff Roses card No 36 – small petite point rose design
- ❧ Madeira rayon 40 embroidery thread: palest apricot 1127, apricot 1053, rust rose 1174, grey green 1306, black green 1394 and cream 1082
- ❧ Monofilament thread
- ❧ Machine feet: clear-view freehand foot and open-toe embroidery foot
- ❧ Size-80 embroidery needle
- ❧ Craft glue
- ❧ General sewing requirements

## PREPARATION

**1.** From the brocade fabric and fusible batting cut 13in x 51in (33cm x 130cm) rectangle. Iron the batting to the back of the brocade fabric using a hot steam iron.

**2.** From the cream fabric cut a 14in x 51in (36cm x 130cm) rectangle for backing the table runner. Cut another piece of fabric 10in x 18in (25cm x 36cm) for the center front of the table runner.

**3.** Iron Vliesofix/Wonderunder to the back of the silk print, the cream fabric for the center of the quilt and the four lace-corner motifs.

**4.** On the long sides of the brocade, measure 7½in (19cm) from each end. Then find the center point of both short ends of the brocade. Use these marks to cut matching 'V' shaped points on either end of the brocade fabric and the backing. Cut a parallel 'V' at either end of the cream fabric for the center of the runner, first measuring 5½in (14cm) from each end.

**5.** Cut out the silk print around the 'print' line on the cream fabric and iron it to the center of the cream fabric for the center of the table runner. Iron the cream fabric with the print centered to the center front of the table runner.

**6.** Iron a corner lace motif to either end of the cream fabric, aligning the corner with the center of the 'V' on either end of the table runner to cover part of the raw fabric edge and extending on either side of the 'V'.

## EMBROIDERY

**7.** Use the antique gold thread, size-80 embroidery needle, open-toe foot, pre-wound embroidery bobbin and stitch No 16 width 2.5 length 0.7 to appliqué around the print, centered on the cream fabric, in the center of the table runner. Stitch No 01, length 1.5 is stitched on either side of the satin stitch.

**8.** Repeat the above for the outside edge of the cream fabric center of the table runner, extending the stitch from either side of the two lace motifs.

**9.** Use the same thread and stitch No 96 to embroider on the inside edge of the above three rows of stitching to form a border on the cream fabric.

**10.** Use black green thread and stitch No 01 length 2.5 to stitch over the diagonal cross hatch and around the oval in the silk print.

**11.** Select the petite point rose design from the Pfaff Roses card No 36 and threads from the materials list to embroider this design on either end of the center cream fabric using the photo as guide to color and position.

## QUILTING

**12.** Use the bond powder technique (page 95) to apply cream backing fabric to the back of the table runner making sure the front is exactly centered over the backing fabric and all corners and points aligned.

**13.** Use the clear-view freehand foot and monofilament thread to straight stitch freehand outline quilt the floral design on the brocade fabric, with matching thread in the bobbin to the backing fabric.

### BINDING

**14.** Press the table runner, and if necessary trim the backing fabric so it extends ½in (1.5cm) evenly on all sides of the runner.

**15.** Bring the backing fabric to the front of the runner, over the raw fabric edges on the right side of the fabric, extending ⅜in (1cm) evenly around the table runner covering all raw edges. Pleat the corners and points to ensure the binding sits flat. Pin in place.

**16.** Use an open-toe foot to straight stitch around the table runner close to the raw fabric edge of the backing fabric, on the front of the table runner.

**17.** Use the open-toe foot, antique gold thread in the needle and bobbin and stitch No 16 width 3.0 length 0.7 to appliqué over the raw fabric edge of the backing fabric around the right side of the fabric on the table runner. Stitch No 01 length 1.5 is then sewn on either side of the satin stitch.

### TASSELS

**18.** Cut the 12in (30cm) wide fringe into two lengths.

**19.** Run glue along the header of the fringe then roll into a tight cylinder. Hold this rolled-up end tightly in your hand and flip the fringe over your hand (inside out), so the fringe falls back over your hand and the rolled header.

**20.** Pull up four strands of fringe from the center of the flipped threads to act as a tie – tie a knot in the ends, then loop this end over a doorknob or similar object.

**21.** Smooth the fringe evenly over the rolled header and secure with matching thread under the knot (rolled header) of the fringe to form a tassel. Make two tassels.

**22.** Stitch these tassels on the right side of the table runner centered in the 'V' on either end.

**23.** Iron a corner-lace motif on either end of the table runner, making sure they are centered in the 'V' and cover the end of tassel.

**24.** Use the clear-view freehand foot, monofilament thread in the needle, matching thread to backing fabric in the bobbin and a straight stitch to freehand stitch around the outside edge of the four lace motifs to quilt and secure them completing the table runner.

# Hat &
# Hat Box

*B*oth the hat and hatbox were made from pre-loved items. You can purchase a box of any shape or size, or make or cover your own, or use these techniques for a cushion or wall hanging. The ribbon roses have many applications, but do look wonderful on this little hat.

# Hatbox

## MATERIALS

*Note: Materials are listed for the embellishments only, not the hatbox. The one used is purchased and has a diameter of 12in (30.5cm) and a height of 5¾in (14.5cm) and has a cord handle.*

- 1 Victorian print 1054 large by Jenny Haskins on cream satin 11in (28cm) square
- 12cm (30cm) fusible batting
- 8in (20cm) Vliesofix/Wonderunder
- 3 hand painted lace motifs in colors reflecting those in the print
- 3⅓yd (3.m) antique ½in (12mm) braid
- Blue/green seed beads, beading needle and thread
- Antique gold tassel
- Madeira rayon 40 embroidery thread: cream 1082 and pale blue green 1047
- Monofilament thread
- Size-80 embroidery needle
- Pre-wound bobbins
- Machine feet: clear-view freehand foot and the open-toe foot
- Craft glue
- Photocopy paper for stabilizer
- Tracing paper, pencil, compass
- General sewing requirement

## PREPARATION

1. Iron the fusible batting to the back of the silk print, trim away spare batting.

2. Use the tracing paper, pencil and compass to draw a circle with a diameter of 9½in (24cm), cut it out, center it over the silk print backed with fusible batting and cut out. From the spare piece of batting, cut another same-size circle.

3. Refer to page 94 in the techniques section to iron the Vliesofix/Wonderunder to the back of the hand painted lace pieces.

## QUILTING

4. Use the open-toe foot and the pale blue green rayon embroidery thread, size-80 embroidery needle, a pre-wound bobbin and stitch No 01 (triple stitch) to quilt the diagonal grid in the center of the heart.

5. Use the above and stitch No 165, width and length 6.0 density 0.25 to embroider over the heart outline using photocopy paper as a stabilizer at the back of the work and the 'dual feed' (built-in compact walking foot) engaged for ease of feeding.

6. Embroider stitch No 62 length 10, width 6.0 density 0.25 in the center of each open rose – single pattern.

7. Use the clear-view freehand foot, straight stitch and cream thread to stipple quilt inside the drawn circle around the printed heart. Use monofilament thread and a straight stitch to outline-quilt the flowers and leaves that surround the heart.

## BEADING

8. Use the seed beads, the hand beading needle and thread to bead around the scallops on the edge of the heart print, on each crossbar of the grid and on the stamens in the center of the open roses.

## PUTTING IT TOGETHER

9. Use the glue to attach the gold braid around the outside edge and the bottom of the rim of the hatbox lid.

10. Center the fusible batting over the lid of the hatbox and glue. Cut around the marked circle that surrounds the beaded heart print, and center it over the fusible batting on the lid and glue, pressing firmly around the outside edges to slightly flatten them. Glue the remaining gold edging braid around the outside edge of the circle covering the raw fabric edges.

11. Cut the lace motifs into suitable individual pieces, then use the photo as a guide to position and glue the lace around the silk print overlapping onto the hatbox lid.

12. Glue the tassel to the center front of the lid, on the rim.

# Hat

## MATERIALS

*Note: For machine embroidery materials and techniques refer to pages 10 to 13 before commencing this project.*

- Choose a suitable hat to decorate
- 3yd (3m) two tone apricot 1½in (4cm) wide wire edged ribbon
- 1½yd (1.5m) rust 1½in (4cm) wide wire edge ribbon
- 2yd (2m) two tone soft blue green 1½in (4cm) wide wire edged ribbon
- Hand sewing needle and beading thread
- 1yd (1m) black hat netting
- 3in (7.5cm) bias strip of black fabric the circumference of the hat brim
- ½in (1.5cm) flat gold braid the circumference of the hat brim
- Victorian Bows and Butterflies signature disk by Jenny Haskins Cactus Punch
- 8in x 16in (20cm x 40cm) Marcia Pollard's heavy-duty soluble-stabiliser
- Rayon 40 embroidery thread cream for the needle and bobbin
- Black construction thread and normal sewing foot
- Size-80 embroidery needle
- 3 small ribbon roses and two butterfly trinkets
- Glue
- General sewing requirements

## ROSES AND LEAVES

1. Refer to pages 98, 101 and 102 for instructions how to make the ribbon roses and leaves. Make two apricot and one rust colored rose and five leaves.

## EMBROIDERED LACE BUTTERFLY

2. Wind two bobbins with the cream rayon embroidery thread and down load Lace Butterfly 1 Small on a blank memory card using PC-Designer software.

3. Place two layers of the heavy-duty soluble-stabilizer in the embroidery hoop and embroider the lace butterfly using cream thread in the needle and the bobbin.

4. When embroidery is complete, cut away excess stabilizer from around the butterfly then wash out the stabilizer in warm soapy water. Rinse, making sure all the stabilizer is removed, and set the butterfly to dry.

## TRIMMING THE BRIM

5. Fold over a narrow hem on either side of the black bias strip of fabric and stitch down with black thread.

6. Fold the bias strip in half lengthwise and press. Place around the brim of the hat so the fold sits on the brim. Glue in place pulling the fabric firmly around so it sits flat. Turn under the raw fabric, overlapping the ends to complete.

7. Glue the gold edging braid over the edge of the black fabric around the brim of the hat.

8. Use the photo as a guide to position the roses and leaves around the hat and glue in place. Glue the lace butterfly and two butterfly trinkets above the roses.

9. Fold over each end of the hat netting 6in (15cm) and gather up, catching down the ends. Use the photo as a guide to place the netting over the roses. Catch it down at intervals, take the gathered ends to the back of the hat and stitch them in place with a hand sewing needle and thread. Scatter the three ribbon roses over the net on either side of the hat, gluing them in place.

10. You may wish to make a decorative hat pin to finish your Victorian bonnet.

# Quilt
## for Narelle

# Quilting

## TECHNIQUES AS OLD AS THE HILLS

*The 'For Narelle' quilt which incorporates quilting, embroidery and broderie perse is a modern day version of quilts from the seventeenth century.*

*Right at the beginning, quilting was simply two layers of fabric, with batting in between, held together with hand stitching. Quilting goes back as far as the Egyptians and was introduced to Europe at the end of the eleventh century by the Crusaders returning from the Holy Wars. The Crusaders had adopted the Eastern style of incorporating quilted fabric in their armor..*

*As bed covers, quilts date from the fourteenth century. Although there are earlier references to quilts in literature, the oldest surviving examples of quilting are a pair made in Sicily for the marriage of members of the Guicciardini and Acciaiuili families in 1395. I found it personally very validating to learn that the techniques I use for machine embroidery have been used on quilts for centuries.*

*The broderie perse technique dates from the seventeenth century with the introduction of polished cottons and chintzes from India. The emphasis moved from needlework on quilts to the application of figurative motifs cut from the chintz and applied on to a solid background with almost invisible stitching.*

*It is also interesting to note that quilting in the early part of the eighteenth century was synonymous with embroidery, with quilts heavily embellished with gold threads and hand stitching.*

*Some people come into your life and pas quickly by, others come into your life for a shor time but stay with you forever – such a person is Narelle Grieve who taught me humility, love and acceptance. This quilt is for her in honor of her encouragement and her absolute belief that I am a quilter.*

**Finished size of the quilt 56in square.**

*Note: Measurements will be given in imperial measurements only in keeping with quilting tradition. Should you find imperial measurements confusing, use a tape measure with both imperial and metric.*

---

### MATERIALS

*Note: For machine embroidery materials and techniques refer to pages 10 to 13 before commencing this project.*

- 64in old gold green 45in wide silk dupion for the blocks, block borders, block sashing and binding

- 84in antique gold 60in wide delustered satin for quilt backing and borders

- 36in antique brocade fabric 45in wide for block borders

- 1-1½yd rose floral fabric suitable for appliqué motifs

- 4 Jenny Haskins Victorian Rose prints – one for the center of each quilt block

- 6½yd antique double edged 3in wide lace for the outside border of the quilt

- 60in square Hobbs Thermore ultra thin batting

- 2 tins Audrey's bond powder

- 1–1½yd Vliesofix/Wonderunder

- Victorian Bows and Butterflies Jenny Haskins signature disk by Cactus Punch

- Victorian Bows and Baskets design disk by Jenny Haskins 'Bow5t'

- Small piece of antique lace to appliqué some of the butterflies

- Madeira rayon 40 embroidery threads: rose pink 1054, dark rose pink 1341, olive green 1157, warm brown green 1191 and antique gold 1338

- Madeira metallic gold No 3

- Monofilament thread

- Machine feet: open-toe foot, clear-view freehand foot, narrow edge foot and ¼in foot

- Machine needles: size-80 embroidery needle, size-75 universal and size-60 sharp
- Photocopy paper for stabilizer
- General sewing requirements

*Note: This quilt is constructed in the traditional way of completing the quilt top by piecing, embroidering then sandwiching the batting between the quilt top and quilt backing and quilting through the whole quilt. Should you choose you could back each block with fusible batting before completing each block's embellishment and quilt as you go which is a much simpler method of achieving a similar effect.*

### PREPARATION

1. From the old gold green silk dupion cut:

—four 15in squares for the blocks

—ten 3in strips across the width of the fabric for block sashing, quilt inner borders and quilt binding

—from the above cut two 21in strips and one 44in strip for sashing strips to join the blocks together.

### FROM THE ANTIQUE BROCADE FABRIC CUT:

—eight 4in strips across the width of the fabric

### FROM THE ANTIQUE GOLD DELUSTERED SATIN CUT:

—50in square for quilt backing
—eight, 4 ½in strips the width of the fabric for quilt borders and backing of borders

### FROM THE HOBBS ULTRA THIN BATTING CUT:

—one 50in square for center of quilt
—four 4 ½in wide strips the width of the batting for quilt borders

2. Iron the Vliesofix/Wonderunder to the back of the floral fabric suitable for appliqué then use the small sharp scissors to cut out floral motifs (for broderie perse around each embroidered block) referring to the photos of individual blocks for guidance.

3. Iron Vliesofix/Wonderunder to the back of the antique lace that is to be used for the butterfly appliqué and silk prints. Cut out around the prints then iron one to the centre of each of the four blocks.

### CONSTRUCTION

*Note: Use the photo as guide to block positions and lay them out on a clean flat surface. Lay the sashing strips between the blocks. Two 21in and one 44in strips of sashing fabric.*

4. Use the ¼in foot, construction thread in the needle and bobbin to join:

—brocade fabric border strips to the top and bottom and then to either side of the four 15in squares

—one, 21in antique gold sashing strip to the right hand side of the two left hand blocks

—the right hand blocks to the left hand blocks along the other side of the antique gold sashing strips (two rows of two blocks joined by a sashing strip down the middle)

—the two-block rows together with the 44in antique gold sashing strip

—the top and bottom inner antique gold border strips, then the sides.

Press all seams to the center.

### EMBROIDERY

5. Embroider the following in the center of the quilt using the photo as a guide to thread color and position:

—'Bow5t' from Victorian Bows and Baskets in the center of the quilt on the intersection of the sashing strips using rose pink and dark rose pink thread

—two 'Butterfly No 4' from Victorian Bows and Butterflies using olive green, warm brown green and dark rose pink thread

—one 'Butterfly No 3' from Victorian Bows and Butterflies using olive green, warm brown green and rose pink thread.

6. Use paper as a backing stabilizer, open-toe foot, size-80 embroidery needle, rayon 40 warm brown green embroidery thread, pre-wound bobbin and stitch No 16 width 4.5 length 0.7 to embroider

around each block, covering the seam where the block border fabric and the blocks meet.

7. Use the photo as a guide to position the cut out roses around each block, remove the paper backing then position the flowers and iron in place using a hot steam iron on the right side of the fabric. Number the blocks one to four from left to right then use the block photos as a guide to color and position and embroider the following:

BLOCK 1

BLOCK 2

BLOCK 3

BLOCK 4

### BLOCK NO 1

—stitch No 55 width and length 6.0, density 0.25 using gold metallic thread around the outside edge of the heart

—three, 'Butterfly No 5', using the lace fabric as an appliqué, on and around the block

### BLOCK NO 2

—stitch No 154, width and length 6, using gold metallic thread around the outside edge of the heart

—three, 'Butterfly No 3' on the block

### BLOCK NO 3

—stitch No 50, width and length 6, using gold metallic thread around the outside edge of the heart

—three 'Butterfly 4' on and around the block

### BLOCK NO 4

—stitch No 62 width 6.0 length 10 density 0.25 and 165 width and length 4 density 0.25, placed in a memory, around the outside edge of the oval

—three 'Butterfly 9' wings and body, using the lace as an appliqué in and around the block.

8. Press the quilt top flat and smooth, stretching as

you press to ensure all the blocks are true to shape and the embroidery is not puckered.

### QUILT BACKING

9. Sandwich the batting between the quilt top and the backing fabric using the Audrey's bond powder technique as found on page 95 to apply the batting to the quilt top then the backing fabric to the underside of the batting. Make sure the quilt top and backing are evenly centered over and under the batting, and that there are no wrinkles.

### QUILTING

*Note: Clear a large area around your sewing machine and fold the quilt into a manageable size to suit the area on the quilt you are sewing. Use thread in the bobbin that best matches the backing fabric at all times and thread in the needle as you are instructed.*

*Note: Refer to page 13 for freehand stipple-quilting and outline quilting. For quilting using the broderie perse technique, see page 97.*

10. Use the narrow edge foot and monofilament thread in the size-60 needle, straight stitch and thread to match the quilt backing in the bobbin to stitch-in-the-ditch in all seam lines.

11. Use the clear-view freehand foot, straight stitch and antique gold thread to freehand stipple-quilt the center sashing strips of the quilt. Change to olive green thread to stipple-quilt the center of the heart in block No 1 using a small stipple-stitch.

12. Use the open-toe foot, stitch No 01 length 1.5 and olive green thread to stitch over all grid lines in the center of the print on blocks 2 to 4.

13. Select stitch No 60 width and length 6.0, density 0.25 and olive green thread to stitch on the outline of the three hearts and oval shapes aligning the straight edge of the stitch with the drawn line of the oval/hearts, and with the scallops facing to the center.

14. Select stitch No 01 length 1.5 and olive green thread to stitch around the straight edge of the above stitch, following the shape of the hearts/oval.

15. Use the clear-view freehand foot, size-60 sharp needle, monofilament thread to freehand:

—straight-stitch outline quilt the flowers, leaves and buds that surround the hearts/oval in the center of each block

—narrow zigzag outline quilt and seal the edge of the fabric rose motifs around each block (Broderie Perse technique, see page 97)

—straight-stitch outline quilt the fabric design on the block brocade border fabric

—straight stitch outline quilt around all machine embroidered motifs on the quilt starting from the center and working out.

**16.** Use the clear-view freehand foot, size-80 embroidery needle, straight stitch and the antique gold thread to freehand stipple-quilt the inside area of each block and the inner quilt borders.

**17.** Use the open-toe foot, stitch No 01 length 1.5 and olive green thread to stitch down either side of the wide satin stitch that covers the block seams with the border fabric

**18.** Use the Bond powder technique to apply the batting to the back of the old gold delustered outer border strips. Then press the quilt and trim the sides, straightening and squaring them if necessary.

**19.** Stitch the side border strips to the right side of the quilt, right sides of fabric together, raw edges aligned stitching from the batting side of the borders.

**20.** Stitch the side backing border strips to the underside of the quilt, right sides of quilt backing and border strips together, raw edges aligned, stitching in the seam-line of the side quilt borders, from the wrong side of the fabric.

**21.** Attach the border backing strips to the underside of the border batting using the Bond powder technique. Make sure all seams are flat and fabric smooth. Trim ends.

**22.** Attach the top and bottom border strips in the same manner as the sides, starting and finishing on the outside edge of the side borders. Press flat and trim each end.

### Attaching the Lace

**23.** Pin the double-sided lace so it covers the seam of the inner and outer quilt borders and is apportioned equally between them. Starting at the inner border, stitch the lace in place using a clear-view freehand foot and a freehand straight stitch to follow the scalloped edge. Pleat both sides of the lace at each corner, clipping between the designs if necessary. Attach the other side of the lace to the outer border in the same way, making sure the lace is flat and smooth.

### Quilt Binding

**24.** Fold the remaining four 3in-binding fabric strips in half lengthwise and press. Attach the binding ½in from the raw fabric edge of the quilt. See Straight Binding technique on page 96 to bind the quilt. You

may choose to use the narrow edge foot and thread in the needle to match the border fabric to stitch-in-the-ditch of the quilt binding from the right side of the fabric to attach the binding to the back of the quilt.

**25.** Name, sign and date your quilt on the right side of the fabric, in the bottom right hand corner of the quilt to complete your masterpiece.

Enjoy this Narelle, this is for you.

*E*verything that is old is new
again as the saying goes. Many of the projects
in this book recycle cherished pieces
that are hard to part with and this shawl is one
such treasure of mine. You can either do as
I have or make a shawl from start – we give you
the materials and instructions.

## Shawl
ᦥᦥ

### MATERIALS

*Note: For machine embroidery materials and
techniques refer to pages 10 to 13 before commencing
this project.*

- Pre-loved shawl or a triangle of lace with two
  sides measuring 46in (117cm) one long side of
  65in (165cm) opposite a right-angled corner

- 2⅔yd (2.5m) of beaded fringing 6in (15cm) wide

- 1 hand-painted corner lace motif

- 5 larger double rose hand painted lace motifs

- 6in (15cm) Vliesofix/Wonderunder

- Victorian Butterflies Jenny Haskins signature
  disk with Cactus Punch

- Madeira Rayon 40 embroidery threads: black,
  teal green 1391, rose pink 1341 and softest
  apricot 1127

- Black construction thread

- Monofilament thread

- Victorian Bows and Butterflies Jenny Haskins
  signature disk Cactus Punch

- Machine feet: normal sewing foot and clear-view
  freehand foot

- Hand sewing needle

- General sewing requirements

### PREPARATION

Those without an embroidery/sewing machine can
achieve a similar effect by adding two lace butterflies
to the lace motifs. Embroidery/sewing machine
owners may choose to embroider Victorian roses and
leaves in place of the hand painted lace motifs – the
choice is yours.

1. If starting with a lace triangle, cut around the lace
motifs on the long side to form a decorative edge or
hem it in your preferred way.

2. See page 94 to attach the Vliesofix/Wonderunder to
the back of the hand painted lace motifs. Cut them

up to suit the placement on the shawl.

3. Iron the lace motifs in place using the photo
as a guide.

### EMBROIDERY

4. Embroider two 'Butterfly 4' from the Victorian
Bows and Butterfly design disk using black thread as
the background and matching the outlines and 'veins'
to the hand painted lace motifs.

### PUTTING IT TOGETHER

5. Attach the beaded fringe to the outside edge of the
sides adjacent to the right-angle, allowing for the
point of the shawl. Use black construction thread
in the needle and bobbin, and use the normal sewing
foot. Hand sew the ends of the fringe to the
underside of the shawl.

6. Use the clear-view freehand foot, monofilament
thread in the needle and matching thread in the
bobbin to the shawl to attach the lace motifs using a
straight stitch that follows the outside edge of the
lace motifs.

## *A* Victorian Brooch
ᦥᦥ

*A* petite Victorian silk rose print, from the
Jenny Haskins collection is the basis for this
romantic little brooch. Hand embroidery, by
Carole Cree, using antique gold thread and tiny
silk ribbon roses gives a three-dimensional effect
to the brooch which is trimmed with a minute
gold braid and antique beaded fringe.

### MATERIALS

- 1 petite Victorian Rose print No 1006 by
  Jenny Haskins

- 3in (7.5cm) square of lightweight batting,
  cardboard and felt for backing

- 1½in (4cm) of beaded fringe 3in (7.5cm) long

- ³⁄₁₆in (4mm) wide silk ribbon in dusky rose and
  deep dusky rose

- Craft glue

- Hand embroidery needle

- Antique gold embroidery thread or two strands
  of Madeira gold No 3 metallic thread

- 8in (20cm) narrow gold metallic trim

- Monofilament thread

- Machine feet: clear-view freehand foot

- General sewing requirements.

# Rose Strewn Accessories

## TECHNIQUE

1. Refer to page 97 and use the silk ribbon to make two dusky rose wound ribbon roses and one deep dusky rose wound ribbon rose.

2. Use the hand embroidery needle and your choice of gold thread to embroider the lattice in the center of the oval, using a long stitch between each cross bar.

3. Place lightweight batting under the embroidered print and use the clear-view freehand foot and monofilament thread to quilt around the marked edge of the oval.

4. Use a fabric-marking pen to draw an oval around the outside edge of the roses that surround the gold embroidery, ¼in from the quilted outline. Use this as a guide to cut the cardboard and felt backing. Cut out the print around the drawn oval leaving a ¼in (6mm) seam allowance for turn to the back of the brooch.

5. Center the embroidered print over the cardboard and glue the print to the cardboard by evenly pulling the clipped edges of the oval print to the back of the cardboard.

6. Carefully glue the gold metallic trim to the outer edge of the stretched print.

7. Fold and glue the ribbon header of the beaded fringe in half to double its density and glue it to the center bottom of the print from the cardboard side. Cover the back of the brooch with the felt oval and glue. Later glue the brooch clip to the center back of the felt.

8. Use the photo as guide to position and color of the ribbon roses and glue in place.

*A vision of shimmering light and sumptuous color, this jacket reflects a past and precious era when romance was always in the air. The beauty of this project is that you can make it from our pattern, use your own favorite pattern, or embellish a jacket that is already in your wardrobe to give it a look that is quintessentially Victorian.*

*Note: The construction of this jacket requires the expertise of a tailor or couturier dressmaker, but the embellishments are very simple to apply to a purchased jacket or one that is already in your wardrobe.*

## MATERIALS

*Note: For machine embroidery materials and techniques refer to pages 10 to 13 before commencing this project.*

- Midsummer Night's Dream jacket pattern from the pattern sheet
- 1⅔yd (1.5m) silk brocade 60in (150cm) wide for jacket
- 1⅔yd (1.5m) lining fabric for jacket
- 1⅔yd (1.5m) Hobbs Ultra-thin Thermore Premier batting for quilting
- ½yd (50cm) woven interfacing for the facing pattern pieces
- 1 antique lace collar
- 1 antiqued lace insertion bib 17in x 8in (43cm x 20cm)
- Madeira rayon 40 embroidery thread: rust rose 1174, deep burgundy 1385, yellow gold 1070, rose gold 1126, black green 1393, warm brown green 1191, antique gold 1338 and mid brown 1144
- Construction thread to match jacket fabric
- Monofilament thread
- Machine needles: size-80 embroidery needle and size-75 universal needle
- Machine feet: open-toe foot, normal sewing foot, quilting guide, zipper foot and clear-view freehand foot
- Victorian Roses CD by Jenny Haskins
- Photocopy paper for stabilizer
- 2yd (1.85m) fine piping cord
- Shoulder pads to suit
- Fray stopper
- Tracing paper and lead pencil
- General sewing requirements

## PREPARATION

1. Use the tracing paper and lead pencil to trace the pattern pieces from the pattern sheet, making sure all pattern pieces are marked and numbered. Cut the traced pattern pieces out using paper scissors.

2. Use the pattern pieces for the jacket to cut from the silk brocade and batting:

—two jacket fronts pattern piece No 1
—two side fronts pattern piece No 4
—one center back pattern piece No 2
—two side backs pattern piece No 5
—two sleeves pattern piece No 3

Use the facing pattern pieces for the jacket to cut from the silk brocade and the fusible woven interfacing:

—two front facings pattern piece No 8
—one center back facing pattern piece No 7
—two side front facings pattern piece No 11
—two center front facings pattern piece No 10

Iron the woven interfacing to the back of brocade fabric facing pattern pieces.

3. Using the pattern pieces for the jacket lining to cut from the lining fabric:

—one center back pattern piece No 6
—two side fronts pattern piece No 9
—two sleeves pattern piece No 3
—two side front pattern piece No 4
—two side back pattern piece No 5

4. Pin the batting to the back of all the jacket pieces, basting at intervals.

## QUILTING

5. Use the quilting guide, open-toe foot with the 'dual feed' (walking foot) engaged, rayon thread to match the fabric, a size-80 embroidery needle and a straight stitch to quilt the following pattern pieces:

—two fronts pattern piece No 1
—one center front pattern piece No 2
—two sleeves pattern piece No 3

using diagonal straight lines that are 1in (2.5cm) apart removing the basting as you sew.

## EMBROIDERY

6. Use jacket brocade fabric to embroider nine 'openrose' designs using the rust rose and deep burgundy thread, ten 'leaf1'and two 'leaf2' using the warm brown green and antique gold thread.

7. Apply the fray stopping liquid to the outside fabric on the edge flowers and leaves taking care not to let it get on the stitching, then use a small sharp pair of scissors to cut around the flowers and leaves close to the edge of the stitching.

8. Use the fabric marking pen and the photo as a guide to draw a rose branch and twigs that extend from the center of the left shoulder down the left front, stopping 2in (5cm) above the marked tie notch on the left front pattern piece.

9. Draw another branch and twigs on the right front from the center of the shoulder that extends 10in (25cm) down the quilted front.

10. Use paper as a stabilizer, open-toe embroidery foot, medium brown thread, a size-80 embroidery needle and stitch No 16 width 3.0 length 0.7, tapering at the ends over the marked branch and twigs on the quilted fronts.

## CONSTRUCTION

11. Cut 1¼in (3cm) bias brocade fabric strips joined to measure 2yd (1.85m) to make the narrow piping for the front and back of the jacket. Encase the fine piping cord in the folded strip of bias brocade then use the zipper foot and needle positions to stitch close to the piping cord on the right side of the fabric.

12. Join the front and back side pattern pieces to the fronts and each side of the back, inserting the piping using construction thread and the zipper foot and needle positions to stitch close to the piping. Clip the curved seam edges. Top stitch these seams on the right side of the side pattern pieces, close to the edge of the piping.

13. Join the fronts to the back of the jacket at the shoulder seams, press seams flat then join the left and right front pattern pieces at the center back, making sure it fits accurately then press seam flat. Join this to the back neck section of the center back of the jacket right sides together, stitching from the wrong side of the fabric.

14. Join left and right front facing pattern pieces together at the center back seam. Attach the joined front facing to the left and right fronts, right side of fabric together stitching from the wrong side of the fabric. Trim and clip all seams then turn to the right side of the fabric, pulling the ties through making sure that the points of the ties are sharp.

15. Attach the center back brocade facing to the center back of the joined front facings, then top stitch the seam on the facing side of the seam.

16. Attach the sleeves to the jacket, leaving the underarm seam open.

**TIP:** *Pin the large lace bib to the center back of the jacket extending from each shoulder and around the back neck. Pin the square antique collar over the bib and around the neck bringing it to the front of the jacket. This allows you to position the roses and leaves so they will not be hidden under any lace pieces.*

17. Use the photo as guide to positioning the leaves then the roses over the leaves on the front and back of the jacket. Pin the leaves first, then use the clear-view freehand foot, monofilament thread and a straight stitch to stitch around the inside edge of the leaves to hold them in place.

18. Pin the roses over the leaves, then stitch in place as for the leaves. Five roses on the left front, one on the right front shoulder. Two roses on the left shoulder and one on the bottom right of the center back quilted panel.

## PUTTING IT TOGETHER

19. Join the lining pattern pieces together and press all seams flat.

20. Join the jacket side seams through to the underarm seam on each sleeve.

21. Attach the center front facing to the left and right front facing pieces of the pattern then the side front facing to the center front facing, matching the notches.

22. Position and stitch the shoulder pads in place.

23. Place the right side of the lining over the right side of the jacket, matching shoulder and side seams, and pin in place. (Remember to stitch a movement dart in the center back lining at the neck and bottom edge.) Pin the lining to the brocade facings on the inside of the jacket leaving a 10in (25cm) opening at the bottom of the center back for turning. Stitch around the edge of the jacket and the lining from the wrong side of the lining leaving the center back opening for turning.

24. Trim then clip all seams and turn to the right side of the jacket. Press all seams flat making sure the lining fits well.

25. Complete the jacket by hand sewing the hem at the bottom of the sleeves and the opening in the center back closed.

26. Top stitch around the entire jacket edge, ¼in from the edge of the jacket.

27. Hand sew the large lace bib to the center of the jacket, attaching it at the shoulders and around the back neck. Place the antique lace collar over the lace bib and around the back neck and down each side of the front lapels of the jacket and stitch in place to complete your Midsummer Night's Dream.

*E*nsure your rôle as the belle of the ball with these exquisite embroidered slippers. When making them, if you keep track of the pieces and make sure you flip one sole to make a right and left foot you'll be surprised at how easy they are. The shoe stuffers make glorious gifts that are fragrant as well as enchanting to behold.

## MATERIALS

*Note: For machine embroidery materials and techniques refer to pages 10 to 13 before commencing this project.*

- 12in (30cm) golden green diagonally pintucked silk dupion 44in (112cm) wide for slippers
- ½ yd (50cm) golden green plain silk dupion 44in (112cm) wide for lining
- 12in (30cm) square black suede for shoe sole
- 14in x 24in (35cm x 60cm) fusible batting (for backing pintucked silk and padding the lining on the sole)
- 2¼yd (2m) wire edged 1½in (4cm) wide green ribbon for ties
- 1⅛yd (2m) silk 1in (2.5cm) wide ribbon for binding seams
- 1⅛yd (1m) gold edging braid ⅜in (1cm) wide
- 4 lace motifs 5in x ¾in (12cm x 2cm) aged using the potassium permanganate dyeing technique (see page 62)
- 2 butterfly trinkets
- Craft glue
- 16in (40cm) self-adhesive tear-away
- 12in (30cm) square of heavyweight cardboard
- Black seed beads, beading needle and thread
- Madeira rayon 40 embroidery threads: deep burgundy 1385, rust red 1174, yellow gold 1070, rose gold 1126, dark olive green 1157, warm brown green 1191 and black green 1393
- Victorian Roses embroidery CD by Jenny Haskins
- Machine feet: normal sewing foot
- Size-80 embroidery needles
- Paper scissors
- Tracing paper and lead pencil
- General sewing requirements

## PREPARATION

1. Use the tracing paper and pencil to trace the slipper pattern pieces No 1, No 2 and No 3 from the pattern sheet then cut out using paper scissors.

2. Use the pattern pieces to cut the following:

—from the cardboard left and right innersoles (omitting seam allowance) from pattern piece No 3

—from the pintucked silk dupion, cut two pattern pieces No 1 front and four No 2 back of slippers (one left and one right of each)

—from the lining silk dupion and the fusible batting cut two each of pattern pieces No 1 to No 3 front, back, and innersole of slippers, omitting the seam allowance of the innersoles, (one left and one right of each)

—from the suede cut two soles from pattern piece No 3 including the seam allowance, (one left one right).

3. Fuse the batting to the back of the slipper fronts and backs on the wrong side of the pintucked silk dupion. Glue the batting to the top of the cardboard innersoles.

## EMBROIDERY

*Note: Refer to the free standing embroidery technique on page 13 to embroider six 'openrose' from Victorian Roses CD (three mirrored) and two 'leaf1' (one mirrored).*

4. The 'openrose' uses the following rayon 40 embroidery threads: rust red and burgundy for the petals, two yellows for the center and black green for the stamens and the center of the rose.

5. The 'leaf1' uses dark olive green and warm brown green. When embroidery is complete, use a small sharp pair of scissors to cut each motif out close to the outside stitching and put to one side.

## MAKING THE SLIPPERS

*Note: Make sure that there is one left and one right of all pattern pieces to make one complete left and right slipper.*

6. With right sides of fabric together, sew the center back seam of the slipper backs and lining pieces, then press the seams flat.

# Silken Slippers
# &
# Shoe Stuffers

7. Cut the green wired ribbon into four 20in (50cm) lengths for ribbon ties. On the right side of the slipper backs, pin the ribbons ¾in (2cm) on either side of the center back seam, to the upper edge of the slipper backs. The end of the ribbon to be attached should align with the raw fabric edges of the curved backs of the heels with the ties draped towards the center back seam.

8. Attach the lining to the slipper toes and backs, right sides of lining and slippers together, and stitch around the squared edge of the instep and curved upper edge of the slipper backs, catching in the ribbons (careful not to catch the ties). Clip seams around curves and in corners, press seams towards the lining then turn to the right side. Top stitch just beside the seam on the lining then fold lining to the inside and press all pieces.

9. Layer the slipper soles (ensuring there is a left and right) — suede sole, cardboard with batting then silk lining. On the lining side, stitch around the edge of each insole to hold all layers together.

10. Cut the narrow gold edging braid in half, and attach to the suede sole of each slipper by stitching the straight edge of the braid over the stitch line on each sole, (scalloped edge to the center) overlapping the raw ends to finish off.

11. Mark the center front of each sole and slipper toe on the right side of the toe and the suede side of the sole. Place the right side of the slipper toe to the suede side of the sole, matching the center fronts and pin.

12. Repeat the above for the slipper heel, overlapping the heel section with the slipper toe section, on either side of the sole. Stitch around the edge of each slipper heel and toe on the lining side of the fabric, following the shape of the cardboard sole. Trim all seams to ¼in and clip curved edges.

13. Roll binding ribbon over the seam so it is equal on both sides of the seam, pin if necessary then stitch down close to the edge of the ribbon over the seam line.

14. Center a lace motif at the back of each heel so it sits equally on either side of the center back seam and either hand stitch or glue in place.

15. Place a lace motif on the outside edge of each toe section of the slipper starting at the overlap — pin then either stitch or glue in place.

16. Use the beads, beading needle and thread, to hand sew beads over the stamens in the center of the roses.

17. Use the photo as a guide to position (remember to mirror the design on one slipper) and position two roses and a leaf on each slipper toe and pin. Place the leaf to the outside edge of the slipper then the second rose, on top of the first rose making sure the roses overlap the inside slipper edge and the top rose overlaps the end of the lace motif on the outside of the slipper. Either glue or hand-sew the embroidery in place.

18. Place a rose at the center back of each heel so it sits above the seam line, pin then either glue or hand-sew in place.

Now you are set for the ball — keep an eye out for Prince Charming.

# Embroidered Shoe Stuffers

## MATERIALS

*Note: For machine embroidery materials and techniques refer to pages 10 to 13 before commencing this project.*

- 12in (30cm) pintucked silk dupion
- 32in (81cm) antiqued edging lace 3in (7.5cm)
- 1⅓yd (1.22m) wire edge ribbon 1½in (4cm) wide
- Small amount of Toyfil to fill the shoe stuffers
- Small bag of lavender to mix with the Toyfil
- Normal sewing foot
- Size-80 embroidery needle
- Victorian Roses CD by Jenny Haskins
- Madeira rayon 40 embroidery thread: deep burgundy 1385, rust red 1174, yellow gold 1070, rose gold 1126, dark olive green 1157, warm brown green 1191 and black green 1393
- Construction thread
- General sewing requirements

## PREPARATION

1. From the pintucked silk Dupion cut out four pattern pieces using the template provided on the pattern sheet.

—1¼in (3cm) bias strip 10in (25cm) long for the piping
—one placket strip for skirt placket

**FROM THE PRINTED COTTON NET TULLE CUT:**

—eight godet panels (printed net tulle godets are available from Judy Wearne on application)

**3.** Use a fabric-marking pen to draw around the front yoke pattern piece centered over the silk rectangle.

**4.** Use a tacking stitch to mark the center vertical front of each silk panel then mark the embroidery position as shown on the pattern sheet.

### EMBROIDERY

**5.** Use the photo as a guide to colors used and embroider 'Bow 3' from Jenny Haskins Victorian Bows and Butterflies signature series disk by Cactus Punch over the center marked position on each of the eight silk panels.

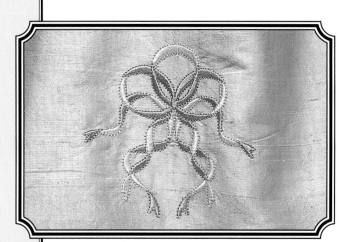

**6.** Use the photo as guide to colors used to embroider design No 220879 (from Jenny Haskins Pfaff Choice card) using the 120 hoop so the design is centered in the outlined yoke on the silk rectangle. The flowers (colors one and two) are embroidered separately in some sections of the yoke to give the effect of scattered flowers.

**7.** When embroidery is complete carefully remove all the excess stabilizer from the back of the embroidery and press all fabric pieces. Then check the pattern piece of the yoke against the outline, adjust if necessary and cut the front yoke out.

### CONSTRUCTION

**8.** Use the silk placket fabric strip to construct a continuous lap placket in the center top of one of the silk panels. This will be the center back skirt panel and opening placket.

**9.** Using your preferred method, overlock (to stitch neaten) each side of the silk skirt panels with a narrow width stitch.

**10.** The skirt panels are pinned together, wrong sides together, and stitched from the right side using a narrow ¼in seam. Press all seams flat on the right sides.

**11.** Join the eight embroidered skirt panels together to the godet insertion mark on each seam, making sure the embroidery is evenly distributed around the skirt.

**12.** Insert the printed net tulle godets between each panel, with wrong sides together, stitching from the right side as for the skirt panels. Press all seams flat, clipping where necessary.

**13.** Use the open-toe foot and size-60/70 sharp needle and matching thread to the lace to stitch the rayon beading lace over the panel seams on the right side of the skirt. Stitch the beading lace down one side only of each of the godets stopping at the point. Use the bodkin to thread the matching insertion ribbon through the beading.

**14.** Stitch the beading lace down the other side of the godet extending it from the hem to the yoke edge of the skirt covering the godet and panel seams and the raw edge of the lace on the other side of the godet.

**15.** Stitch the lace down close to the scalloped edge, making sure it sits flat and straight. Use the bodkin to thread the ribbon through the lace on each panel leaving a ¼in tail at each end.

**16.** Fold the skirt in half around the yoke edge, centering the back placket then cut out the underarm for each sleeve.

**17.** Overlock the hem of the skirt following the scalloped hemline, then turn a narrow hem to the front of the skirt and stitch down – press hem.

**18.** Attach the double-sided edging lace to the hemline of the skirt, with wrong side of lace to right side of skirt, stitching from the right side of the lace. Attach following the hem edge, not the top scallops of the lace.

**19.** Use the beading needle and thread to sew a seed pearl on the peak of each scallop of the edging lace to hold the scallops up and keep the lace attached to the skirt fabric.

**20.** Join the lining and yoke pattern pieces at the shoulder seams, press seams flat and open.

**21.** Join the yoke lining to the yoke by folding the back yoke and lining down the center back, right sides of yoke and lining together, and stitching around the neck edge from the wrong side of the fabric.

**22.** Trim the seam and clip the curved neck edge of the yoke, then turn to the right side and press.

**23.** Use the bias strip of fabric, fine piping cord and zipper foot to make the piping, stitching close to the edge of the cord. Use the zipper foot and needle positions to attach the piping to the front yoke along the bottom edge. Place right side of piping to right side of yoke fabric with raw fabric edges of yoke and piping aligned and stitch from the wrong side of the piping.

**24.** Gather up the skirt to fit the yoke, matching the center front, center back and underarms to the matching positions on the yoke.

**25.** Pin the gathered skirt to the yoke, keeping the yoke lining free, then stitch close to the piping on the yoke front and the bottom edge of the yoke back to the folded center back opening.

**26.** Gather up the head of the sleeve to fit the armhole and the bottom edge of the sleeve to fit the armband. Stitch the sleeve band to the bottom of the sleeve – right sides of fabric together stitching from the wrong side of the sleeve band fabric. Join the underarm seam on the sleeve including the armband fabric.

**27.** Pin the sleeve to the yoke around the armhole matching the center top of the sleeve to the shoulder seam and stitch in place, right sides of yoke and sleeve together, stitching from the wrong side of the sleeve. Trim and clip seam.

**28.** Turn up a seam allowance on the arm-band of the sleeve, then turn up the arm-band to cover the gathered edge of the sleeve and use the hand sewing needle to slip stitch down.

**29.** Turn under a seam allowance on the raw edges of the yoke lining, pin over the gathers of the skirt and sleeves and use a hand sewing needle and thread to slip stitch in place.

**30.** Sew three small buttons and matching buttonholes to the center back of the yoke.

**31.** Hand-sew the double-sided edging lace over the armband of the sleeve to complete you heirloom Victoria Alexandrina christening robe.

Not only is this gown magnificent but practical as well because all seams are either to the front of the gown or covered, eliminating the need for a petticoat and making it lighter and cooler for that new treasured baby.

# Keepsake Box

*This exquisitely painted and embroidered Victorian Keepsake box
was designed and created by Francis Robinson and the team from
Lugarno Craft Cottage.
The box was especially designed for Victorian Roses and is crafted
with an insert recess for the Victorian print which has been embellished
with diminutive hand embroidery and beading
in keeping with the character of the print.
Using single thread French knots, lazy daisy leaves and clusters of antique seed beads
the Victorian Rose print is resplendent in this guided box. See page 103 for kit details.
The Victorian miniature jug and basin are by Delia Clough.*

# The Rose in History

The rose was either born from the smile of Cupid or combed from Aurora's tresses according to Roman legend. In America, Europe and Asia, fossils of rose plants millions of years old have been found. This most celebrated and popular cultivated plant which in turn became the most commonly used adornment of the civilized world certainly existed eons before the appearance of man.

The area once known as Babylonia, cradle of western civilization, was the original rose garden of antiquity. The plants which are native to the Northern Hemisphere, moved west with the successive civilizations that ruled the ancient world. By the seventeenth century the West had its own roses with the Centifolias (Cabbage Roses) arriving a little later. But these early roses usually flowered only once in summer, and briefly at that, with blooms that were usually pink, white or a dull red. Even so, roses were still scarce and a Dutch woman commissioned Jan Breughel the Elder to paint a still life of the flowers she could not afford to buy.

China was more richly endowed with beautiful wild roses than any other country and this led to adventurous rose breeding programs many centuries ago. The colors and scents of the cultivated roses in China and how they flowered over and over again astounded early travelers from the West.

The Victorian era was an exciting age of discovery and development in every field, so it is hardly surprising that there was also a dramatic growth in rose varieties. Very active rose breeders were responsible for this increase. They were quick to track down the latest imported specimens, compare notes amongst fellow rosarians and set about the task of improving their stock.

Early in the nineteenth century, Tea Roses, which had made the long journey from China and survived, were regarded with awe. When they bloomed their flowers were a delicate pastel shade and their fragrance was reminiscent of the inside of old tea chests. But the flower stems were weak and the bushes were not hardy. Some later imports provided shapely buds and high centers; characteristics that remain much prized by rose breeders today.

The popular Victorian rose was the Hybrid Perpetual which had large, fragrant blooms but rampant growth and cumbersome flower shape.

By 1880 it was crossed successfully with the stronger descendants of the Tea Rose to give a better-shaped flower, less rampant growth and improved color range. Thus the Hybrid Teas were born starting with the now world famous 'La France' in 1867.

The late 1800s witnessed the arrival of the yellow roses of Persia. The Persian Yellow helped to produce roses bearing many blooms in an infinite range of shades from palest cream to deepest orange. Not only were colors and petals becoming more plentiful but also the rose had improved from being a mid-summer flowering plant into one that could bloom from early spring well into winter.

The general interest in roses, whether grown or in decoration, increased during Victoria's reign. The voluptuous Cabbage Rose was prominent in Berlin woolwork and was seen everywhere; on fenders and footstools, braces and bell pulls, waistcoats, slippers and every conceivable keepsake or decorative object. Its distinctive pink blooms, echoing the period's predilection for romance and frilliness, appeared constantly; fresh from the garden, embroidered, woven and fashioned from silk, worn on hats, in the hair or in the corsage.

The printed Valentine reached its height of popularity in the closing chapter of the Victorian era. These passionate declarations of devotion and love, scribed with verse and decorated with roses, must have accounted for much of the postman's load.

As the era came to its end, the majority of rose motifs appeared in fairly humble situations: etched on the glass of bars and public houses, cast into coal–hole covers, woven into lace curtains, painted on canal boats and printed on tiles. And although they were plentiful and mass-produced, they are now highly prized by collectors.

The Victorian rosarians would certainly approve of the advances in rose breeding today. Browse the web for roses, old and new, and you'll be amazed with the results. There are more colors, more blooms per plant and more petals per bloom than ever before. Blooms hold longer, flowering seasons are lengthy, perfume is a priority, and plant shape and disease resistance have greatly improved. The rose, it seems, maintains its role as the Queen of flowers.

# Victorian Teddies

The combined talents from the team at Lugarno Craft Cottage festoon these Victorian teddies with a silk satin crazy patchwork collar and tie embellished with gold metallic thread, machine embroidery stitching, hand painted and dyed laces, petite Victorian prints and sparkling dragonfly pins. This is a wonderful way to dress up that tired Teddy who is much cherished and restore him/her to their rightful prominence in your Victorian home.

*Indulge yourself in the pleasures of a bygone era by creating works of art with ribbons and threads on silk prints. The print provides a foolproof guide for all your stitching and the placement of blooms, leaves and buds. What could be easier!*

## Heart Print with Wound Ribbon Roses

### MATERIALS

- Victorian medium size silk print No 1053 by Jenny Haskins designs
- 2¼yd (2m) rose pink Hanah 1in (2.5cm) bias ribbon for roses
- 1⅛yd (1m) green Hanah 1in (2.5cm) bias ribbon for leaves
- Green stranded thread to match ribbon for leaves
- Madeira Metallic thread, Astro, for French knots
- Size-13 chenille embroidery needle for ribbon
- Size-8 milliners needle for French knots
- Frame to suit the size of the silk print
- 24in (60cm) olive green chenille and silk ribbon trim to frame the print
- Madeira Rayon 40 thread to match chenille trim
- 12in (30cm) fusible batting to back the print
- Craft glue
- General sewing requirements

### PREPARATION

1. Follow the step-by-step illustrations and text on page 97 and make two wound ribbon roses.

2. Refer to the photos on page 72 to make four leaves and two wound ribbon rose buds with green calyxes.

### INSTRUCTIONS

#### HAND EMBROIDERY

3. Using the milliners needle and metallic thread, stitch a French knot on each dot around the intersections of the grid on the print. To reduce the fraying of the thread, work with a short length and make sure you thread the end that comes off the reel and knot the end that you cut.

### RIBBON WORK

4. Attach the leaves to the print with a hand sewing needle and thread and small catch stitches, folding under the trimmed leaf bases as you go.

5. With stranded thread to match the leaves, add central and branching veins.

6. **For stitched leaves:** cut a 2in (5cm) length of green ribbon. Create a hole in the print with a large needle at the position of the leaf tip. Thread one end of the ribbon into the chenille needle and pull through the hole in the fabric from the wrong side to the right side. Work another hole for the leaf base and proceed as before but from right side to wrong side of fabric, pulling the ribbon through until ribbon stitch is leaf-like in appearance and the raw edges are folded under the leaf and out of sight. Use hand sewing needle and thread to stitch the ribbon ends together at the back of your work and trim to neaten.

7. **For buds:** Trim raw ends of buds close to the binding thread. Using the same technique and materials as the stitched leaves, make a very small stitch to secure buds on the print. Pull on the stitch firmly to shape the bud base. Stitch ribbon ends together and neaten as before.

8. **For roses:** Make a 'bed' of four or five stitched petals, using the same technique as for the stitched leaves. Sit a wound rose on the bed of petals and attach it to the print with a hand sewing needle and thread. Complete all roses in this way.

### FINISHING

9. Center the print over the fusible batting and with a steam iron on silk setting, carefully press the two together.

10. Arrange chenille trim around the print area in a square and machine stitch in place with small straight stitch and thread matching trim in the needle.

Have the print framed with a border of lace just inside the gilt frame as another pretty addition.

*BUD*

*BUD WITH CALYX*

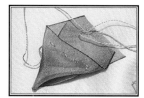

*MAKING A FOLDED LEAF*

*FINISHED FOLDED LEAF*

*WOUND ROSE*

*FOLDED LEAF*

*STITCHED LEAF*

*STITCHED PETALS*

*BUD WITH CALYX*

*POSITIONING THE WOUND ROSE IN THE STITCHED PETALS*

*WOUND ROSE*

# Heart Print with Old Fashioned Roses

## MATERIALS

- Victorian medium size silk print No 1054 by Jenny Haskins designs

- 1⅔yd (1.5m) rose Hanah 1in (2.5cm) wide bias ribbon for roses

- 1⅛yd (1m) green Hanah 1in (2.5cm) wide bias ribbon for leaves

- 1⅔yd (1.5m) antique edging lace 3in (7.5cm) wide to frame the picture

- 12in (30cm) fusible batting to back the print

- Gilded frame to suit size of print

- 1 bundle of dark stamens

- Size-13 chenille embroidery needle for ribbon

- Size 9 crewel hand embroidery needle

- Hand sewing threads to match the silk ribbons

- Craft glue

- General sewing requirements

*Note: This is an exercise in making old fashioned ribbon roses: the leaves are the folded variety from the previous project with a few stitched ribbon leaves beneath the half rose at the lower point of the heart. See page 74.*

1.  Make five folded leaves with green bias ribbon (pictured above left). Using the photo as a guide, stitch them into position on the print, folding under the raw ends as you go.

2.  Using the same technique employed for the folded leaves, make five petals for each rose. Trim the base of each of excess ribbon. With hand sewing needle and thread, stitch the petals around the center of each rose, folding the trimmed ends under as you go.

3.  Working from the back of your work, bring the threaded needle up through the petal and fold the petal tip under to give a rounded shape. Secure the thread on the back of the work.

4.  Fold two or three stamens in half and stitch securely at the base of each petal.

5.  Make the center puff by running a gathering thread in a circle on a square piece of ribbon. Pull the thread to gather it and push the raw ends of the ribbon into the puff to pad it. Stitch this into position over the rose center.

6.  **For the half rose:** Stitch three petals and stamens as above to the print. Stitch a fourth petal over the stamens and add to this a green ribbon base as in the

*Heart Print with Old Fashioned Roses*

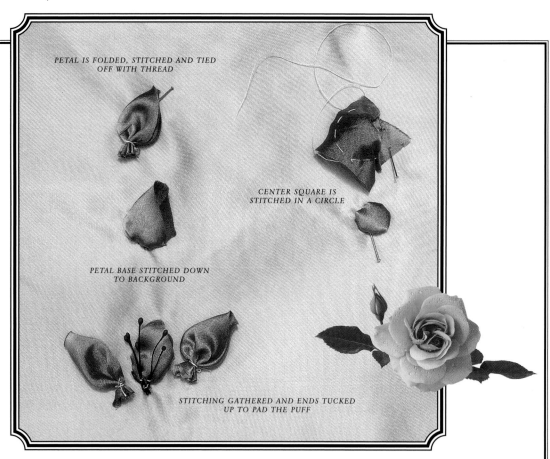

PETAL IS FOLDED, STITCHED AND TIED
OFF WITH THREAD

CENTER SQUARE IS
STITCHED IN A CIRCLE

PETAL BASE STITCHED DOWN
TO BACKGROUND

STITCHING GATHERED AND ENDS TUCKED
UP TO PAD THE PUFF

*MAKING AN OLD FASHIONED ROSE WITH BIAS RIBBON, SEE PAGE 72*

bud base in step No 7 of the previous project. Then stitch three leaves below the base using the stitched ribbon leaf technique.

7. Before framing, back your work with fusible batting (see step No 9 of previous project) and edge it with the lace, gluing the top and bottom strips first and then the sides.

## Captured in Miniature

*Stunningly simple this miniature by Carole Cree of Flights of Fancy is the epitome of beauty in its simplest form. The Victorian print is embellished with hand dyed ribbon, seed beads and a small piece of antique braid.*

### MATERIALS

- 🍃 1 Petite Victorian Rose print by Jenny Haskins No 1054
- 🍃 Small piece of batting to suit the above
- 🍃 Hand dyed Thread Gatherers silk ribbon to match the color of the roses and leaves
- 🍃 Silk ribbon embroidery needle
- 🍃 Seed beads, beading needle and thread
- 🍃 Small pieces of fine antique lace
- 🍃 Glue
- 🍃 Suitable elaborate frame

Use the photo as a guide and refer to the stitch guide on page 98 using the Thread Gatherers silk ribbon and a ribbon stitch to embellish the open roses and leaves.

Hand bead the intersections of the center grid using the beading needle and thread.

Glue the antique braid around the edge of the heart and the fine pieces of lace to cover the print line on the silk. Back the embellished print with the batting and frame to suit your decor.

Captured in
Miniature

ace has a rich past and, with its many fans and followers, will no doubt
have a formidable future. Lace speaks of beauty and innocence, of
frivolity and finesse, of luxury and labor, of fortunes made and lost. Did it
really begin with a rose and a pledge of love? Legend has it that in medieval
times, a knight, before riding off to war, presented his ladylove with a full-blown
rose. As the days passed, she watched and pined for him whilst the rose faded and its
petals tumbled. So determined was she to preserve the symbol of her true love, that
as each petal fell, she stitched it back in place with a needle and thread. In the end
she was left beholding not just a withered rose, but the tracery of her delicate stitches
and thus, a piece of lace.

This story may well be mythical but archeologists found evidence of what must have
been the earliest surviving net lace in the tombs of Egypt. The netting, some of which
was strung with porcelain beads among the meshes, was used for hair nets and partial
garments which were most probably precursors of string vests. It is interesting to
note that these first examples of lace were somewhat utilitarian but as the art of lace
making developed, it became principally decorative; an intriguing fabric that divided
its substance between air and thread—revealing and concealing at the same time.

Much later on, Henry II of France employed lace rather cleverly by commanding a
ruff to hide scars on his neck. His courtiers copied the idea and soon lace ruffs were
the height of fashion. They certainly framed an aristocrat's face to perfection as
portraiture of the day attests. Even some of the stricter member of the breakaway
protestant sects could not resist a flourish of lace at throat and cuff to set off a severe
serge jacket. Lace, because of the interminable hours it took to make a fragment, was
outrageously expensive and therefore the preserve of the rich. Those who could
afford it were determined to wear it with pride and display their worth. But as well
as being worn on the person, lace trimmed the bedchambers of the well-to-do with
canopies, pillow covers, valances, sheets and coverlets. So glorious and extravagant
were these settings that ladies lay in bed during the day and entertained callers (ladies
and gentlemen, both) midst a swirl of lavish lace.

Whereas knitting and the knitters' guilds were the preserve of men, lace making was
nearly always a womanly art. Nuns, small girls and women of all ages had the manual
dexterity and patience to sit for hours and interpret intricate patterns. But the
lacemakers themselves rarely invented these patterns; they were created by artists and
craftspeople who worked in the wider field of the decorative arts. Vinciolo, the
seventeenth century Venetian, set a new standard in beautiful lace designs. His
patterns were widely copied by lesser lacemakers as well as other people such as

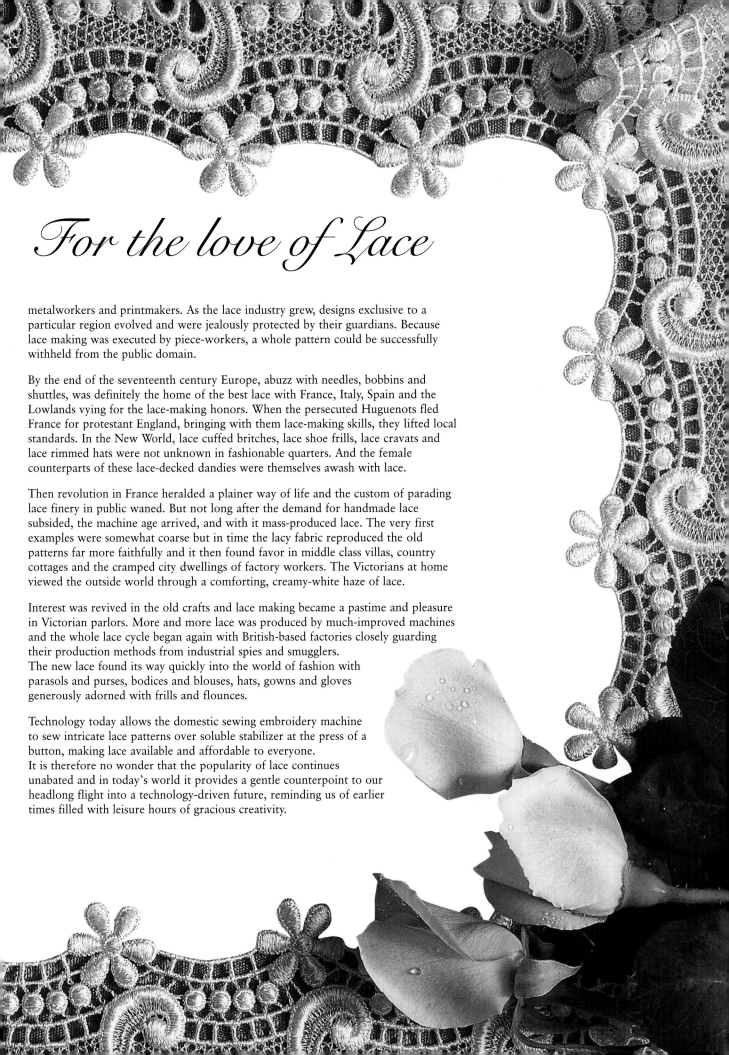

# For the love of Lace

metalworkers and printmakers. As the lace industry grew, designs exclusive to a particular region evolved and were jealously protected by their guardians. Because lace making was executed by piece-workers, a whole pattern could be successfully withheld from the public domain.

By the end of the seventeenth century Europe, abuzz with needles, bobbins and shuttles, was definitely the home of the best lace with France, Italy, Spain and the Lowlands vying for the lace-making honors. When the persecuted Huguenots fled France for protestant England, bringing with them lace-making skills, they lifted local standards. In the New World, lace cuffed britches, lace shoe frills, lace cravats and lace rimmed hats were not unknown in fashionable quarters. And the female counterparts of these lace-decked dandies were themselves awash with lace.

Then revolution in France heralded a plainer way of life and the custom of parading lace finery in public waned. But not long after the demand for handmade lace subsided, the machine age arrived, and with it mass-produced lace. The very first examples were somewhat coarse but in time the lacy fabric reproduced the old patterns far more faithfully and it then found favor in middle class villas, country cottages and the cramped city dwellings of factory workers. The Victorians at home viewed the outside world through a comforting, creamy-white haze of lace.

Interest was revived in the old crafts and lace making became a pastime and pleasure in Victorian parlors. More and more lace was produced by much-improved machines and the whole lace cycle began again with British-based factories closely guarding their production methods from industrial spies and smugglers. The new lace found its way quickly into the world of fashion with parasols and purses, bodices and blouses, hats, gowns and gloves generously adorned with frills and flounces.

Technology today allows the domestic sewing embroidery machine to sew intricate lace patterns over soluble stabilizer at the press of a button, making lace available and affordable to everyone. It is therefore no wonder that the popularity of lace continues unabated and in today's world it provides a gentle counterpoint to our headlong flight into a technology-driven future, reminding us of earlier times filled with leisure hours of gracious creativity.

Gloria's
Whimsical
Whatnots

*Scattered with ribbon and fabric roses, both great and small, these whimsical accessories for a fair lady's boudoir capture the extravagant mood of the nineteenth century.*

## Victorian Pompadour Doll

### MATERIALS

- Porcelain half doll
- ½yd (50cm) off white diamond pin tucked silk dupion
- 2¼yd (2m) rose pink Hanah ½in (12mm) bias silk ribbon to make three wound roses, five rosebuds and seven bound rosebuds
- 1⅛yd (1m) green Hanah ½in (12mm) bias silk ribbon to bind the buds and make the leaves
- 1⅛yd (1m) soft pink Hanah 1in (25mm) bias silk ribbon to tie around the waist of the lady
- Toyfil stuffing
- Quilting thread
- Hand sewing needle
- General sewing requirements

### PREPARATION

**1.** From the silk dupion cut a circle 19in (48cm) in diameter.

**2.** Using quilting thread and hand sewing needle, sew two rows of ½in (12mm) long gathering stitches around the edge of the silk circle. Pull up the gathers and fill the resulting puff quite firmly with Toyfil. Place the doll in the center gathered opening and pull up the gathers tightly around waist of the doll ensuring the raw edges of the fabric are turned to the inside and tie off. Use the 1in (25mm) pink ribbon to tie around the waist of the doll finishing with a bow at the back.

**3.** Make three wound roses (see page 97), and five rosebuds (see photos following Heart Print with Wound Ribbon Roses, page 72). Make seven small rosebuds by winding ribbon without folding it down, cut it, stitch at the base, wrap base in green ribbon and secure with stitches. Make four small rose leaves referring to Heart Print with Wound Ribbon Roses photos. Glue or stitch the flowers and leaves into a trailing bouquet with roses on top surrounded by rose buds and leaves with small buds tapering to a point.

# Teacup Transformed

*A* favorite teacup
without its saucer need not be
a domestic dilemma. When a breakage
leaves you with an orphaned cup,
transform it into a glamorous home
for hatpins and brooches.
Use purchased leaves and flowers
as well as wound roses and
folded rose leaves which you make yourself
to create a cupful of Victorian magic.

## MATERIALS

- Small piece of velvet, brocade or satin with a diameter 4in (10cm) larger than that of the cup or bowl
- Bias silk ribbon of your choice to make three wound roses
- Bias silk ribbon of your choice to make five folded leaves
- Silk ribbon of your choice to make ribbon loops
- Silk ribbon floral braid the diameter of your cup
- Velvet leaves
- Purchased flowers of your choice
- Teacup, mug, bowl (without the lid) or suitable dish
- ½ cup of white rice
- Craft glue or glue gun with three glue sticks
- Hand sewing thread and needle
- Toyfil stuffing
- Quilting thread
- General sewing requirements

## PREPARATION

1. Refer to page 97 for instructions on making the wound roses and to the photos on page 72 of the Heart Print with Wound Ribbon Roses for guidance to make folded leaves. Knot the ribbon for the loops at 2in (5cm) intervals and set aside.

2. Heat the rice in the microwave to kill any 'unwelcome guests' then pour the rice into the cup to weight it. Rice should come to just over halfway up the cup.

3. Cut a circle of fabric 2in (5cm) larger than the diameter of the cup

## INSTRUCTIONS

4. Using quilting thread in the hand-sewing needle, run a gathering stitch around the outer edge of the fabric circle. Center a ball of Toyfil in the fabric circle and pull up the thread around it. Continue to stuff in more Toyfil until the ball becomes quite firm, then pull the gathers up so the ball sits snugly in the top of the cup over the rice. Tie off gathering threads. Glue into position in the cup then refer to the photograph, glue braid around the cup's edge.

5. Arrange all flowers and leaves in a pleasing group with the leaves at the base. Loop the knotted ribbon around your arrangement to make loops and trails. Glue the arrangement to one side of the padded top.

# Potpourri Bag

**3.** From the 8in (20cm) bias strip, cut a piece to measure 16in (40cm) on its longer side then cut this in half [two 8in (20cm) strips]. Attach these to the top end of the front and back of the bag, right sides together, raw fabric edges aligned and stitching from the wrong side of the fabric.

**4.** Remove the beads from ¼in (6mm) from each end of the tape of the bead fringing. Using the zipper foot, stitch tape to the bottom edge of one bag piece, right sides together, edge of fabric and top of header tape aligned and bead fringe angled towards the top of bag.

**5.** Join the bag front and back, right sides of fabric together, raw fabric edges aligned, beads secured with pins away from the bottom seam and stitching down one side, across the base and up the other side from the wrong side of the fabric. Neaten all seams. Turn to the right side of the bag, turn the bias facing to the inside of the bag and press.

**6.** Hand stitch the silk flower braid around the base of the bag just above the beads.

## BOW AND ROSE

**7.** Join the remaining three bias strips together to make one long length. Fold lengthwise with right sides together and stitch to form a tube. Turn to the right side and finger press the seam.

**8.** Refer to the photographs for the bias ribbon rose on page 99 as a guide for making the rose. Because of the bulk of the fabric, there is no need to twist the bias tube at any time to create fullness — just stitch the lower edge, gather and roll up after forming the initial tightly rolled center. To finish, fold down the raw edge to the outside and stitch down.

**9.** For the bud, make the center as for a bias ribbon rose, then turn down the end edge and stitch. Wind sufficient green bias ribbon around the base of the bud to make a calyx (see photo on page 72 of the bud with calyx for the Heart Print with Wound Ribbon Roses).

**10.** Make two folded ribbon rose leaves, referring again to the photos on page 72 of the Heart Print with Wound Ribbon Roses.

**11.** With a hand sewing needle and thread, attach the rose, bud and leaves to the lower right hand corner of the bag front. Fill bag with potpourri mix.

**12.** Use the leftover bias tube to make a tie to secure the bag, cutting each end on the bias then folding in a hem and hand stitching. Turn the facing down to show the diagonal strips.

## MATERIALS

- 30in (76cm) striped silk dupion 45in (115cm) wide for bag and rose
- 8in (20cm) bead fringing for bottom of bag
- 18in (46cm) silk ribbon floral braid trimming for bottom of bag
- 16in (40cm) green 3in (7.5cm) Hanah silk/satin for bud and leaves
- Construction thread
- Machine needle size-65 sharp
- Normal sewing foot, zipper foot
- Hand sewing needle
- General sewing requirements

## PREPARATION

**1.** Use diagram on the pattern sheet as a guide to cutting the silk fabric. The 8in x 30in (20cm x 76cm) silk fabric is first cut in half to measure 8in x 15in (20cm x 38cm) for the front and back of the bag with the stripes running vertically.

**2.** Cut out bias strips for ribbon rose, buds and bag facing strip and put to one side.

*A stunning example of the Victorian maxim
'there is never too much' this lidded porcelain powder bowl is topped with
masses of tiny silk ribbon roses. It is also a wonderful way to use up those
small pieces of silk ribbon that are too good to throw away.
Refer to page 97 on how to make wound ribbon roses, and make sufficient to
cover the lid of the powder bowl so the roses are tightly clustered together –
the number will depend on the width of the ribbon and how tightly you wind
the rose. Then glue to the lid of the powder bowl.*

## Rose-topped Powder Bowl

*T̶his totally over the top
Victorian silk cushion
is as luxurious to touch as it is
to the eye, drawing both senses
to it like magnet.*

**Finished size of cushion is a 12in (30cm) square,
not including the crochet ribbon edge.**

## MATERIALS

- 14in (30cm) of black Hanah silk satin fabric
- 2⅔yd (2.4m) Gloria McKinnon's black crochet ribbon fringe
- 2¼yd (2m) of pink Hanah 3in (76mm) bias silk ribbon for each rose
- 8in (20cm) of green Hanah 3in (76mm) bias silk ribbon for each leaf
- Small amount of crinoline for securing the roses
- Chenille stem for shaping leaf
- 12in (30cm) cushion insert
- Construction thread in black
- Normal sewing foot
- Size-60 sharp machine needle
- Hand sewing needle
- General sewing requirements

*Note: Use ½in (12mm) seams as the silk satin fabric of the cushion tends to fray.*

**1.** Cut two 13in (33cm) squares from the silk satin. Zigzag the edges to prevent fraying. Stitch, right sides together, leaving an 8in (20cm) opening for turning on one side. When stitching the corners, divert slightly inwards to give a better shape when the cushion is filled. Clip across the corners and turn to the right side.

**2.** Ease the insert into the cover. Close the opening with hand stitching.

**3.** Hand stitch the fringe around the outside edge of the cushion (there are two rows). The first row follows the seam along the edge of the cushion. The second row sits ¾in (2cm) above the first on the right side of the cushion. Finish the ends by hand.

See page 99 for instructions for making the Luxurious Rose and 101 for the Luxurious Leaf.

Sumptuous
Silky Cushion

Crisp white voile with hand stitched shadow work, single strand grub roses surrounded by a sash of machine embroidered shadow appliqué and finished with a lace edge stitch, this cushion combines time honored hand embroidery with the magic of 21st century technology.
(See www.jennyhaskins.com for instructions for this cushion.)

This cushion exhibits beauty in its simplest form. Make it from your fabric collection and the silk roses you inherited from grandmother's hope chest. The cushion is edged with a gold cord and another length of it is looped and tied under the roses on the front of the cushion. Fill it with lavender or potpourri.

Victorian rose print, centered on batting backed voile is machine quilted, is embellished with silk ribbon French knots sewn by hand and hand beaded Fluttering butterflies from Victorian Bows and Butterflies, Jenny Haskins signature disk with Cactus Punch, surround the center cushion panel.
(See www.jennyhaskins.com for instructions for this cushion.)

Cream muslin cushion (opposite) features machine embroidery from the Roses card No 36, stitched into a heart shape and surrounded with myriad hand sewn French knots. This piece shows the versatility of quilter and textile artist, Carol Warren.
(See page 103 for details on Carol Warren.)

# Collectors Editions

❧·❧

$C$ome with me on a guided tour
of some exceptional projects and see what can be done
with prints and plain fabrics, handwork and machine embroidery
and something as simple as a looped length of gold cord.
Victoria would be enchanted with them all.

Cherub like faces framed with old-world roses peep through lush foliage of Victorian splendor.
Carole Cree uses hand dyed Thread Gatherers silk ribbon, beading and antique rose petal to embellish these silk prints by Jenny Haskins (No 1002 girls and 1022 roses).
See page 98 for the ribbon stitch and French knots and page 103 for details on Carole Cree.

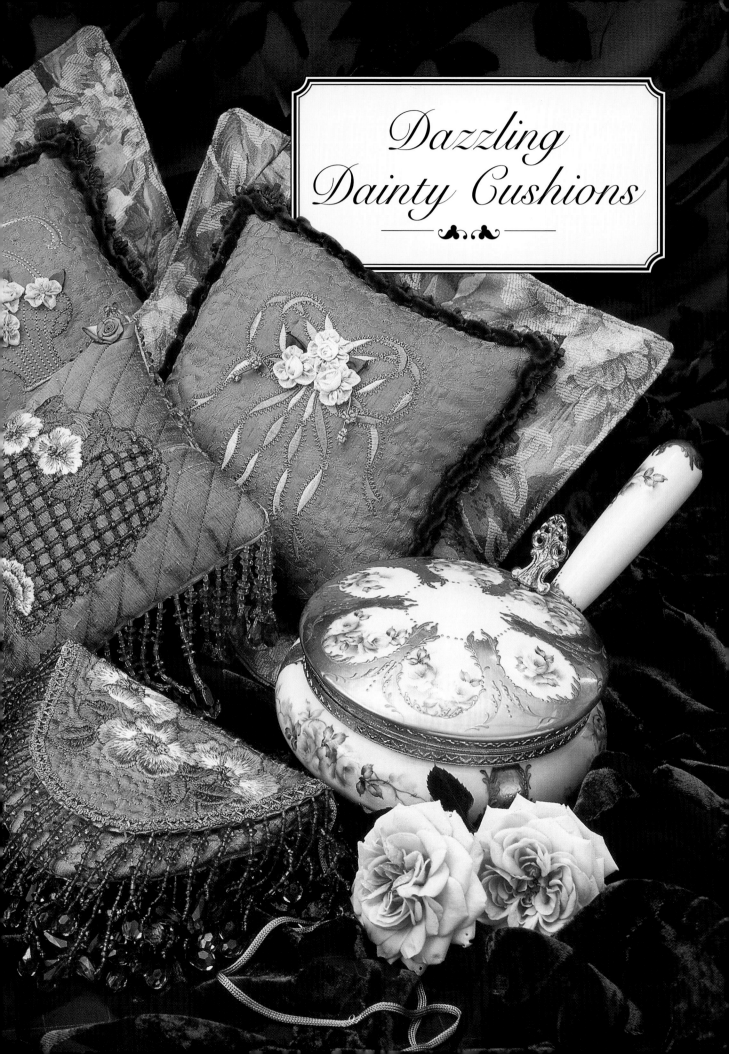

# Dazzling Dainty Cushions

*hese little treasures combine a machine-embroidered bow and basket which is embellished with petite antique ribbon roses and leaves. This is a wonderful way to use the embroidery motifs you test sew after purchasing a new embroidery card as well as those small treasures of fabric you cannot bear to part with.*

**Finished size of cushion 11in (28cm) square.**

Materials given for one cushion, materials should be changed according to the number of cushions being made.

## MATERIALS

*Note: For machine embroidery materials and techniques refer to pages 10 to 13 before commencing this project.*

- 11½in (29cm) floral brocade fabric for border and backing fabric
- 8in (20cm) square of silk brocade for center fabric
- 12in (30cm) square of Hobbs Ultra thin batting
- 1⅛yd (1m) hand dyed rayon ribbon ½in (12mm) wide
- 4in (10cm) green Hanah bias silk ribbon ½in (12mm) wide for leaves
- Chenille needle for silk ribbon embroidery
- Victorian Bows and Baskets design disk by Jenny Haskins 'Bow1p'
- Madeira rayon 40 threads: pale rose pink 1142, rose pink 1054 and antique gold 1338
- Machine feet: normal construction foot and clear-view freehand foot
- Size-80 embroidery needle
- 1yd (1m) chenille and silk ribbon ½in (12mm) braid
- Small amount of cushion filling
- General sewing requirements

## PREPARATION

**1. FROM THE FLORAL BROCADE FABRIC CUT:**

—one, 11½in (29cm) square for cushion back
—two, strips 2½in x 8½in (6cm x 22cm) top and bottom borders
—two, strips 2½in x 11½in (6cm x 29cm) side borders

**FROM THE SILK BROCADE CUT:**

—one, 8in (20cm) square for the cushion front center

**FROM THE BATTING CUT:**

—one, 11½in (29cm) square to back the cushion front

## MACHINE EMBOIDERY

**2.** Use the threads from the materials list to embroider 'Bow1p' in the centre of the silk-brocade fabric square.

## CONSTRUCTION

**3.** Join the 8½in (22cm) floral brocade fabric strips to the top and bottom of the embroidered panel then join the side border strips.

**4.** Pin the batting square to the back of the cushion front.

## QUILTING

**5.** Use the clear-view freehand foot, antique gold thread and a straight stitch to stipple-quilt the embroidered center panel and outline the bow.

**6.** Pin the 11½in (29cm) cushion backing to the cushion top, right sides together, raw edges aligned stitching from the wrong side of the fabric.

**7.** Stitch around all sides, leaving a 5in (13cm) opening for turning.

**8.** Turn the cushion to the right side and press the seams. Pin the cushion top to the cushion backing on the outside edge of the embroidered panel then use the normal foot to stitch around the center panel leaving an opening to match the border opening.

**9.** Place the cushion filling in the center of the cushion, pin the embroidered panel opening then stitch the opening closed along the seam line.

**10.** Turn the seam allowance in to the wrong side on the border opening, pin then top stitch around the edge of the border fabric closing the turning opening.

**11.** Stitch the chenille trim around the seam line on the center-embroidered panel and the border fabric strip.

**12.** Make up three rayon ribbon roses, each with five full-blown outer petals and a tighter but flattened center. The background petals are stitched and gathered up first (see page 102) and attached to a small piece of crinoline. The buds do not have rolled edges as in cabochon rosebuds but are made from a loosely rolled coil of rayon ribbon. Make a coil of five or six 'rounds', squash it, weight it and when it stays squashed, stitch it to the center of the five petals with down-in-the-ditch stitches, which should not be discernible from above. Make two folded leaves referring to the photos for the Heart Print with Wound Ribbon Roses on page 72. Use the photo as a guide to position and hand sew the leaves under the roses positioned in the center of the embroidered bow.

**13.** Antique Forget-me-not trim extends on either side or you may choose to embroider small blue flowers to substitute for this fabulous and rare trim.

The second cushion is made in the same manner as the first using 'Basket2' from Victorian Bows and Baskets by Jenny Haskins, with the same machine embroidery thread colors and fabrics. Similar ribbon roses and leaves fill the machine embroidered and embellished basket.

The beaded bag, square cushion with bead fringe and lace-frilled and beaded heart cushion are miniatures of beauty and grace. Although they are made using designs from Victorian Roses design disk they look like hope chest booty from more than a century ago.

# Techniques

## MACHINE FEET

Pfaff sewing machines have a compact built-in walking foot called a Dual Feed. The Dual Feed clips into the back of the sewing machine foot and feeds the fabric from the top while the feed dogs move the fabric from the underside ensuring perfect feeding of fabric regardless of fabric thickness or type. The Dual Feed is ideal for quilting, piecing and for stitching built-in stitches over several layers of fabric giving perfect results every time. This built-in foot is exclusive to Pfaff sewing machines so should you not have a Pfaff then purchase a walking foot to suit your sewing machine.

*NORMAL SEWING FOOT*

*ZIPPER FOOT*

*CLEAR VIEW FREEHAND FOOT*

*OPEN TOE FOOT*

*1/4 INCH FOOT*

*NARROW EDGE FOOT*

One thousand meter reels of rayon 40 thread tend to unravel and create havoc in the workbasket. A simple solution is to secure them with crossed-over rubber bands.

## APPLYING VLIESOFIX/WONDERUNDER TO THE BACK OF LACE

If the above products appear in the materials lists of any projects in this book, always proceed as per the instructions given below.

**There are three ways of applying lace to fabric:**

—sewing by hand or machine around the lace edge with either a matching or monofilament thread using a freehand technique
—gluing in place using a strong glue such as 450 which is suitable for craft projects that are not going to be washed
—ironing to the fabric using a double-sided fusible web (Vliesofix/Wonderunder).

**The first two methods are self-explanatory and the third is explained here in easy steps.**

1. Place a piece of paper on the ironing board. Place lace pieces wrong side up on top of paper.

2. Cut a piece of Vliesofix/Wonderunder the same size as the paper and place over the lace, rough side facing down, paper side up.

3. Use steam and heat to iron the Vliesofix/Wonderunder to the back of the lace ensuring that the excess web is ironed to the paper.

4. Allow to cool before removing the paper side of the web. The lace will now be covered with a fine web and the excess will adhere to the paper.

5. Remove the lace from the paper, then pull away any excess web from around the edge of the lace. The small amounts of web trapped in the holes of the lace can either be pulled away by hand or will melt away when next ironed.

*TIP: Fusible web is a heat and steam-dissolving bonding agent, so use plenty of steam. If your iron does not generate enough steam, then lightly mist the lace with water before applying heat, To prevent the web sticking to the iron, use an appliqué mat.*

*[1] LACE WRONG SIDE UP ON PIECE OF PAPER*

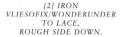

[2] IRON
VLIESOFIX/WONDERUNDER
TO LACE,
ROUGH SIDE DOWN.

[3] WHEN COOL, REMOVE
PAPER.

## BACKING PRINTS AND FABRIC WITH VLIESOFIX/ WONDERUNDER AND FUSIBLE BATTING

Vliesofix/Wonderunder (fusible web) and fusible batting bond to fabrics when steam and heat activate the bonding agent.

Place the print/fabric, right side up, over a same size piece of either the fusible batting (bonding side up) or double sided fusible web (rough side up) and apply steam iron. Peel away backing paper of fusible web before steam ironing it to fabric.

The right side of prints can be steam ironed, but if you are a little nervous, use an appliqué mat over or under the print.

*Note: Never iron the right side of the print directly onto the ironing board as fluff or lint may stick to the print. Use either an appliqué mat or a clean lint free piece of cotton cloth over the ironing board.*

## AUDREY'S BOND POWDER

A wonderful way to avoid pinning through all layers of a quilt and to prevent puckering during the final stages of assembly is to quilt through with Audrey's Bonding Powder.

**1.** When the quilt is pieced, cut the quilt backing up to 2in (5cm) larger on all four sides than the actual quilt.

**2.** Before applying the quilt backing, place quilt front right side down on the ironing board, batting facing up if you are using a fusible batting.

**3.** Lightly sprinkle Audrey's Bond Powder onto the batting, place quilt backing over batting making sure you center it and press in place with a hot iron. Work your way down the quilt ensuring the fabric is square and even. The bonding powder lightly fuses the quilt backing to the batting so that you can quilt through with ease, eliminating the need to pin. Should the fabric move, a light press with a steam iron will re-bond it.

**4.** You can also use the same technique should you choose to use a non fusible batting, by applying the bonding power to attach the quilt top on one side and the backing on the other.

## MITERING CORNERS

Mitering corners is joining fabric at a 45° angle to form a square edge (90° angle). It can be daunting, but need not be. There is a simple way to succeed every time with ease and confidence and the following steps will guide you. The photos refer to lace, but the same technique can be used in fabrics for cushions, tablecloths and patchwork.

**1.** When planning a mitered corner, lay the lace/fabric on a flat surface, right side up, to create the desired corner, overlapping the strips to be mitered by the width of the strips of fabric/lace being joined. The top strip is A and the bottom strip is B.

**2.** If you are attaching this to another piece of fabric/lace then pin this to the edge of the fabric, allowing for the overlap to miter the corner. Stitch the fabric/lace to the edge of the fabric starting and finishing 6mm (¼in) on either side of the corner.

**3.** Fold the end of strip A back and under until the end of the A fabric/lace strip is aligned with the underside edge of strip A and over strip B.

**4.** Press and pin the fold line.

**5.** Turn to the wrong side of the fabric/lace strip and pin along the fold line with right sides of strips together.

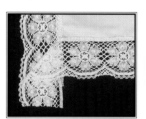
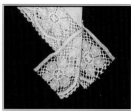

[1] DETERMINING
FOLD LINE OF LACE

[2] PIN ALONG LACE FOLD
LINE ON WRONG SIDE

[3] CHECK FOLD LINE
ALIGNS WITH HALF-CORNER
FOLD OF FABRIC

[4] ON WRONG SIDE,
TRIM MITER SEAM AFTER
STITCHING

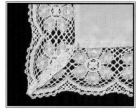

[5] FROM RIGHT SIDE,
ZIGZAG OVER MITER SEAM TO
SECURE LACE

6. To check that the angle is correct, if you are joining fabric/lace to another fabric, fold the 90° angle of the corner (of the fabric that is being joined onto) in half to form a 45° angle. The pin line and subsequent seam line should be an extension of the fold line, thus forming a straight line. Sew a seam along the pinned line from corner to corner.

7. From the wrong side, trim the excess fabric from strips A and B to a ¼in (6mm)-seam allowance for fabric and as small as possible for lace then press the seam open.

8. If working with lace, turn to the right side of the lace and sew over the seam with a small zigzag stitch to secure the raw edges of the lace on the wrong side.

## QUILT BINDING

Cut the quilt binding fabric either on the straight or bias, according to your preference.

As the binding is folded in half lengthwise before it is stitched, allow a generous width, say around 4in (10cm).

### BIAS BINDING

1. Cut the fabric on the bias. A good method of doing this is to fold a fabric square into a double thickness triangle. Bias is on the long side. Fold this long side in half. With rotary cutter on mat, cut into four-thickness strips. Remember to allow for ¼in (6mm) seams and the center lengthwise fold.

2. Join the bias pieces in one continuous strip, always joining them on the straight grain of the fabric to avoid a bubbled seam (the join will be at a 45° angle to the edge of the strip).

3. Iron this strip in half lengthwise, with the wrong sides and the raw edges together.

4. Cut strips of Vliesofix/Wonderunder no more than 1in (2.5cm) wide. Iron this (paper side uppermost) to the edge of the bias strip so that it sits exactly on the folded edge; this will now be the wrong side of the quilt binding. Do not peel the paper from the back of Vliesofix/Wonderunder as the sticky surface revealed tends to be a nuisance when you machine stitch.

5. Round the corners of the quilt then pin the binding, with wrong side of the binding facing up and the raw fabric edges of the binding and quilt aligned, to the right side of the quilt. Attach the binding to the quilt with a straight stitch, using an open-toed foot with the Dual Feed attached (or a walking foot) allowing a ¼in (6mm) seam allowance.

6. Join the binding by turning under the raw edges of one end of the bias strip and slipping the other end into the fold; seam through all layers.

7. Peel the paper from the back of the Vliesofix/Wonderunder and fold the binding over to the wrong side of the quilt so the folded edge (with the Vliesofix/Wonderunder residue beneath it) just covers the row of stitching just completed. Iron in place using a hot steam iron, working on all four straight sides first and leaving the corners to last.

8. Ease the curve with your fingers just prior to pressing with the iron. This will hold permanently without stitching. You may choose to stitch-in-the-ditch from the right side with transparent thread to add extra strength to the binding.

*[1] CUTTING BIAS STRIPS WITH ROTARY CUTTER*

*[2] JOINING STRIPS ON STRAIGHT GRAIN OF FABRIC*

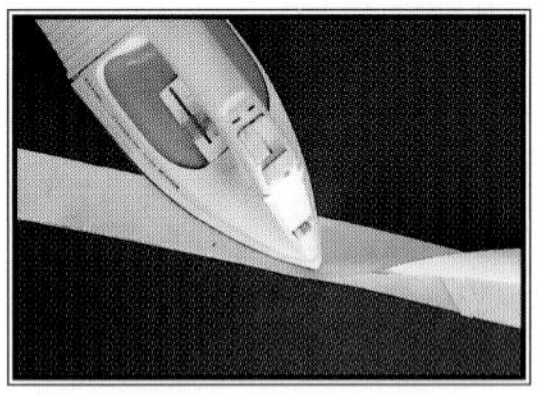

*[3] FOLDING IN HALF LENGTHWISE, WRONG SIDES TOGETHER*

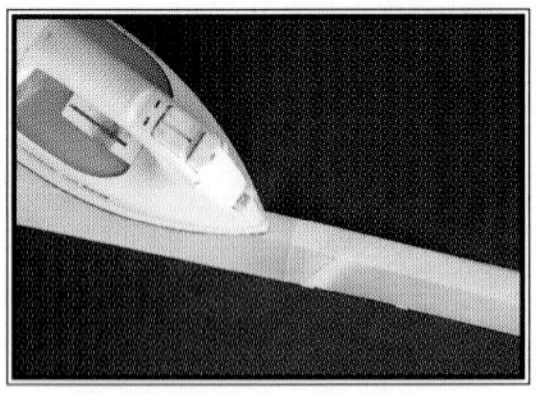

*[4] IRONING FUSIBLE WEB STRIP TO FOLDED EDGE OF FABRIC*

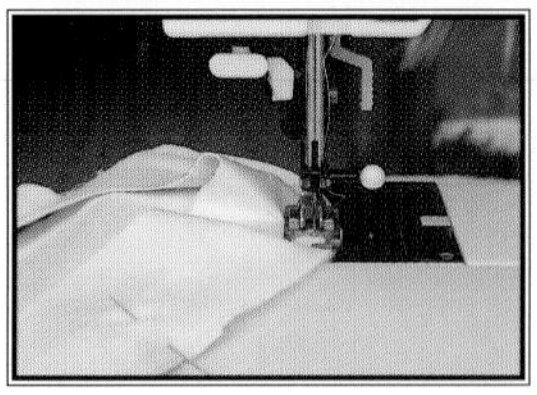

*[5] STITCHING TO QUILT EDGE, PAPER IS STILL ON WEB STRIP*

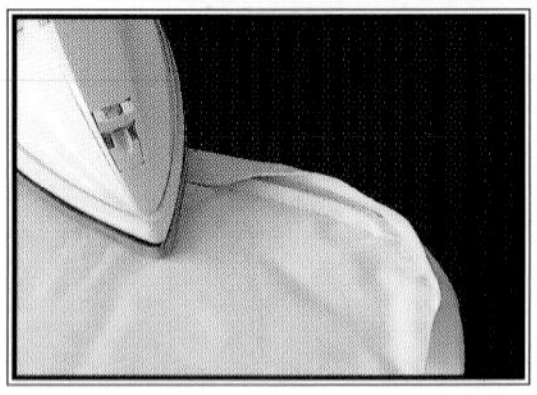

*[6] IRONING BINDING IN PLACE. DO CORNERS LAST*

### STRAIGHT BINDING

Straight binding is attached in four separate pieces; two opposite sides first, then the top and bottom.

1. Cut the fabric on the straight and join if necessary. Fold lengthwise as in the bias technique. You will need at least 3in (7.5cm) longer than each side.

2. Treat with Vliesofix/Wonderunder (as above) and attach the binding to either side of the quilt (as above), then remove the backing paper from the Vliesofix/Wonderunder. Fold binding to the back of the quilt and iron as before. Trim the binding ends level with the quilt.

3. Work from the right side of the quilt centering the top and bottom binding strips over the quilt, with the raw edges of the binding aligned with the raw edges of the quilt. Fold the 1½in (3.5cm) overhangs to the back of the quilt and pin before attaching the binding as before, stitching though all layers of fabric.

**4** Fold the binding up, then iron a small piece of Vliesofix/Wonderunder to the underside fabric of the fold and peel away the backing paper.

**5** Fold over the binding strips and press in place as before. You may choose to stitch-in-the-ditch as before to finish the binding, but this is not necessary.

### PAINTING ROSES

All my rose fabric prints and my rose machine embroidery designs started out as paintings. These were converted to paintings on fabric, which I further embellished with embroidery and lace. After they proved to be popular in my classes, I had them printed on a variety of fabrics such as silk organza, silk dupion, delustered satin, net and moiré grosgrain. If you want to experiment with painting roses, start on paper first to perfect your technique. Beginners often appreciate a bit of help at the start so enlarge the basic shapes below by 200% and trace over them. Use my color combinations as a guide. There are many famous botanical illustrations of roses which you could track down in your local library or bookshop and also use as a starting point for your own works of art. When you are confident enough to paint on fabric, keep the fabric taut and stable by stretching it over a piece of cardboard and securing it with adhesive tape.

### BRODERIE PERSE

Broderie perse involves attaching cut-out fabric motifs to a base fabric with very fine, almost invisible stitches. The motifs' edges are sealed and attached to the base fabric with either a straight stitch or narrow zigzag to give a 'seamless' result (as opposed to appliqué which has a very defined edge.)

Apply a double-sided fusible web to the back of the fabric to be cut out. Cut out carefully around the edge of the design to be applied to the base fabric. Fuse the cut-out design to the base fabric. Use a clear-view freehand foot and monofilament thread, a zigzag stitch and a size-60 sharp needle to seal the edges of the cut-out design. Using the size-60 sharp needle ensures that the stitching is almost invisible to

the naked eye. In the case of the For Narelle quilt, the broderie perse is quilted through to not only seal the edges of the cut out design but also to outline quilt at the same time.

### MAKING A TWISTED CORD

**1.** Measure out 12yds (12m) of black rayon thread then double it up until it measures 1½yd (1.5m) keeping the ends even. Set up the machine in bobbin winding mode, then place one end of the black threads through the center of the bobbin and place the bobbin on the winder with the threads secured through the center.

**2.** Hold the free end of the threads out from the sewing machine, so the threads are taut, then engage the bobbin winder; this will twist the threads. Keep winding until you feel the threads pull back towards the bobbin. Take the end of the threads in your hand to the bobbin, folding the length of twisted cord in two, and secure the fold with your other hand. Carefully remove the threads from the bobbin, keeping a tight grip on the threads in both hands – one hand on either end of the twisted cord. When the threads are released they will twist back on themselves forming a cord. Knot the free ends securely to ensure the cord remains twisted.

### WOUND RIBBON ROSES

**1.** Draw the raw edge down a little then roll the ribbon three or four times around it to form the center of the rose. Secure with a few stitches, pic 1.

**2.** Fold the ribbon on the cross; each fold becomes a petal. See pic 2.

**3.** Pull the center of the rose down when you roll the ribbon around it so the top of the fold is level with the center. Stitch the base of the rose after each fold.

**4.** Keep folding and stitching until you have the size and shape you want. A few folds will make a bud. Lots will make a full blown rose. See pic 3.

1          2          3

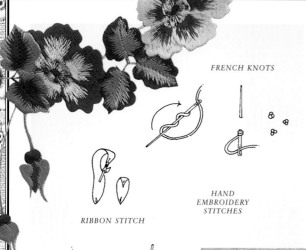

FRENCH KNOTS

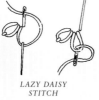

HAND
EMBROIDERY
STITCHES

RIBBON STITCH

LAZY DAISY
STITCH

## Gathering Wire Ribbon

Pin your starting tail (as in the case of the gathered wired ribbon roses below) firmly to the arm of an upholstered armchair. The pinned, folded and closed tail will prevent the wire from being dislodged from the lower edge of the ribbon. From the other end of the ribbon, pull out sufficient wire to wrap around a small pair of scissors or seam ripper. Hold the scissors in your right hand (left if you are left-handed) and work on the ribbon with your other hand. With the wire stretched taut, ease a handful of ribbon from the scissors end towards the pinned tail until it stops. Work on another handful of ribbon, down the line from the first. Close the gap between the two ruffles by easing the first handful down to the second. Continue in this way until the length is gathered to your satisfaction, then cut off all but 2in (8cm) of the pulled-out wire.

A COLLECTION OF WIRED RIBBON ROSES

---

### RIBBON TIPS

#### Measuring Lengths for Wired Ribbon Roses

The aim, when making wired or unwired ribbon flowers, is to achieve a naturalistic fullness in relation to the width of the ribbon itself. To this end, the increment for measuring ribbon is the width of the ribbon (referred to as WR in the following instructions). All the lengths that are cut are multiples of the width. For accurate measuring in order to ensure that the petals achieve life-like fullness, mark out the exact width of your ribbon between two pins, and use this gauge to measure lengths before cutting.

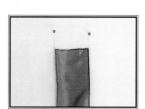

[1] USE TWO PINS TO
ESTABLISH WIDTH OF RIBBON

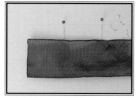

[2] THEN MEASURE OUT
LENGTH OF RIBBON
REQUIRED

#### Supporting Blooms on Crinoline

Crinoline is a stiffened open mesh to which ribbon is stitched. You can substitute lightweight buckram or folded stiffened net for crinoline. Whatever you use, this supporting mesh allows you to add 'air' between rounds of gathered ribbon resulting in a more naturalistic result with open petals as opposed to the tighter appearance when outer rounds are always stitched to the inner 'core'. Trim excess crinoline back to the anchoring stitching when the flower is finished.

## Gathered
## Wired Ribbon Roses

### MATERIALS

- 36 WR of 1½in (38mm) wired ribbon

- Scissors reserved specifically for cutting through wired ribbon

- Pins

- Large needle and non-slip hand-sewing thread such as quilting thread or buttonhole twist to match ribbon

- Small piece of crinoline

*Note:* With this rose, shaded ribbon has been used with the lighter pink to the inside, which gives the finished flower an intriguing inner glow. Reverse the sequence for subsequent blooms for an interesting effect when the roses are grouped.

1. Fold down the end of the ribbon to make a tail.

2. Close over this fold.

3. Start to roll tightly from the closed over vertical edge.

4. Roll to enclose the long selvedge of the first fold and pin.

5. Pin to crinoline.

6. Make a couple of tucks in the lower edge and re-pin.

7. Gather up the lower edge of the wire (see gathering wire ribbon, above). Encircle the center with the gathered ribbon, using a needle and knotted thread to secure the gathered edge firstly to the core with its tail and then to the crinoline.

8. At the end, take the outer edge of the ribbon down to the level of the gathered wire so the raw edge will be hidden. Tease out the ruffles with your fingers.

# Luxurious Bias Ribbon Rose

❧ 2¼yd (2m) of pink Hanah 3in (76mm) bias silk ribbon for each rose

❧ Small amount of crinoline for securing the roses

❧ Hand sewing needle and neutral thread

1. Thread needle with a good length of neutral thread. Roll ribbon for about 8in (20cm) to create a center. Stitch at base to small square of crinoline to secure.

2. Twist the ribbon so the outer edge comes into the center and stitch to crinoline. Do this a total of three times to make fullness.

3. Use the same thread to stitch about 8in (20cm) along the bottom edge of ribbon, gather up and stitch at base. Continue in this way until all the ribbon is used, but just before reaching the end, stitch in a curved line up to the top edge so the cut edge will be hidden when the thread is gathered. Gather up and stitch securely to the crinoline. Trim away crinoline to a suitable size.

[1]

[2]

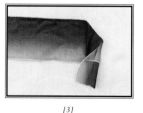
[3]

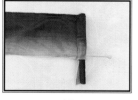
[4]

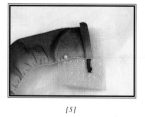
[5]

[6]

[7]

[8]

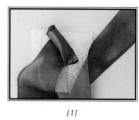
[1]

[2]

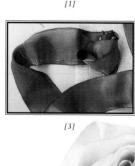
[3]

# Luxurious Bias Ribbon Leaf

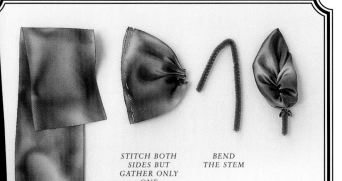

STITCH BOTH
SIDES BUT
GATHER ONLY
ONE

BEND
THE STEM

LEAF SUPPORTED
BY STEM AND
FASTENED OFF

FOLD RIBBON
TO MEASURE 4IN
(10CM )AND CUT

- 8in (20cm) of green Hanah 3in (76mm) bias silk ribbon for each leaf
- Chenille stem for shaping leaf cut to 6in (15cm)
- Hand sewing needle and neutral thread

1. Fold ribbon in half to measure 4in (10cm) in length.

2. With right sides together (the right side is the shiny side), stitch along one edge and fasten.

3. Stitch along the other side and gather up the stitching, keeping the needle and thread attached.

4. Bend chenille stem 2in (5cm) from the end and fit into leaf with gathered seam at center front and the curve of the stem supporting the leaf shape.

5. Wrap and stitch the ends around the stem. Fasten off.

# Wired Ribbon Boat Leaf

This leaf has gathers at its base and is smooth at the tapered top.

## MATERIALS

- 10 WR of 1½in (38mm) wired ribbon
- Pins
- Needle and non-slip hand-sewing thread such as quilting thread or buttonhole twist to match ribbon

1. Place ribbon horizontally before you and fold in half to measure 5 RW.

2. Turn down upper corners at both ends to make a 45° angle and pin. The shape is now similar to an up-turned boat.

3. Mark a point two thirds of the way up the diagonally folded right hand side. Starting ⅛in (3mm) from the point on the right with a knotted thread and well secured double stitch, stitch up to the mark and at this point sew a back stitch. Then continue to the point on the other corner. Draw up the gathers – the back stitch will stop the gathering.

4. Turn the leaf through to the right side, adjust gathers if necessary and knot your thread to fasten off.

[1] FOLD RIBBON
IN HALF

[2] FOLD DOWN CORNERS
AND PIN

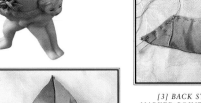

[3] BACK STITCH AT
MARKED POINT AND STITCH
AROUND STEM

[4] OPEN OUT, ADJUST
GATHERS, KNOT THREAD
TO FASTEN OFF

## Wired Ribbon Leaves

Make these from two ribbon-width lengths of any width of wired ribbon.

1. Remove wire from one side of ribbon. Cut piece to measure 2 RW in length.

2. Establish the center of the ribbon length and fold down at the point from the wired side.

3. Fold the other side down.

4. Hand stitch along the bottom.

5. Pull up and wind thread around leaf bottom and stitch through to secure.

(Photos show right side of leaf.)

[1] FOLD RIBBON
IN HALF

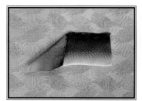

[2] FOLD DOWN CORNERS
AND PIN

[3] BACK STITCH AT
MARKED POINT AND STITCH
AROUND STEM

[4] OPEN OUT, ADJUST
GATHERS, KNOT THREAD
TO FASTEN OFF

[4] OPEN OUT, ADJUST
GATHERS, KNOT THREAD
TO FASTEN OFF

# Small Five-Petal Flower

### MATERIALS

- 12½ RW length of ribbon
- Hand sewing needle and thread
- Anti-fray product
- Dressmakers pencil
- Scrap of crinoline

1. Cut ribbon across the grain and fray ends and trim to ensure your cut is aligned with the grain.

2. Apply the anti-fray to ribbon ends when working with narrow ribbon such as ⅜in (9mm).

3. Leaving ⅛in (3mm) at each end, divide the ribbon into five equal sections by folding. Mark the outer edge at these divisions with the pencil.

4. Stitch as shown in the diagram, with rounded corners, firstly knotting and backstitching at the start ⅛in (3mm) from the end.

5. After completing the stitched outline of the first division, note the side on which the needle came out at the selvedge. The needle must start its next 'journey' on the opposite side on the ribbon so the selvedge is enclosed.

6. Complete the stitching, always dealing with the selvedge as described in step 5, and draw in the thread tightly, back stitch and knot but don't cut the thread. Instead, stitch into the first backstitch to close the circle.

7. Stitch the five petal flower to crinoline, anchoring it with tiny stitches at the center.

[1] 12½ RW LENGTH HAS
BEEN STITCHED

[2] STITCHING THREAD
IS GATHERED AND SECURED
TO MAKE A FIVE-PETAL
FLOWER

# Credits

The eminent artists listed below generously contributed their time and talents to this publication.

**Delia Clough** of Rosarium (Latin for rose garden) is an accomplished artist specializing in finely made jewelry and collectibles.
The hand-sculpted roses with which she decorates her work linked perfectly with the theme of *Victorian Roses* and the figurines especially created by her for this publication have been used in several of the photographs (see below and right). Delia's preferred medium is bisque porcelain, her inspiration is led by spiritual and environmental concerns and her creative direction is forged by her love of all things beautiful. Contact Delia on phone 61 8 9293 1457 fax 61 8 9293 0450 web site **www.rosarium-deliaclough.com**

**Carole Cree**, from Flights of Fancy brings to the 21st century all the charm and grace of the Victorian era. Carole, well known at craft shows where her work is much sought after, has been featured in *Victoria*, the benchmark magazine for Victoriana enthusiasts. Carole's love of beautiful hand embellishment techniques speaks for itself and is seen on pages 51, 75 and 88. Kits for these projects and others are available. Contact Carole on phone 1 817 491 4681 Email: cjcreejr@earthlink.net

**Gloria Mckinnon** and the team from Anne's Glory Box produce unique creations with fabric, thread and lace resulting in Gloria's Collection of soft romantic treasures that will grace any home that is Victorian at heart. Gloria is a lady who has an aura of Victorian splendor that lights up a room upon her entrance. She is the author of more than dozen books and is a feature artist in many international publications and makes regular TV appearances. See pages 70-73, 78-85 — kits are available for these projects, contact Gloria on phone 61 2 4961 6016 fax 61 2 4961 6587 web site **www.textiletraders.com.au/agb.htm**

**Jane Nesbitt** is the National Training Manager for Pfaff American Sales Corp and is well known for her organizational skills at the Pfaff North American Dealer Conventions (in particular, the classes). New product training around the US and coordinating and training the education consultants are also part of Jane's job specifications. It is fitting therefore that Jane be part of *Victorian Roses* where we see her creative skills also, see pages 3 and 38 for her contribution. Contact Jane on JBNesbitt@aol.com.

**Francis Robinson** and the team from Lugarno Craft Cottage are well know for their exquisite works of art covering a whole range of techniques and mediums including découpage, folk art, stenciling and many creative textures. Francis and team have written many books as well as being regularly featured in magazines in Australia. See pages 66 and 69, and for kits to complete these projects contact Francis on phone 61 2 9584 1944 fax 61 2 9533 1485 web site: **www.lugarnocraft.com.au**

**Carol Warren** of Carol's of Midland is a textile artist and quilter who has a passion for color and design and realizing the creative power of machine embroidery, combines it with quilting, hand embroidery and heirloom sewing, see page 87. Carol's work has been featured in many quilting and machine embroidery magazines and is well known for her inspirational classes.
Contact Carol on phone 61 8 9250 2722 fax 61 8 9250 2721 email: warren@argo.net.au for information on her kits and classes.

**Judy Wearne** of the Heirloom Studio set in country New South Wales is surrounded with soft voiles, crisp linens, delicate laces, the rustle of silk and the swish of lace. Judy's gentle, loving nature is reflected in her exquisite and original heirloom christening gowns, one of which is featured on page 62. Traveling the country to teach, lecture and write feature articles for craft magazines Judy still finds time to constantly change her range of products, adapting them to suit the place and times. Contact Judy on phone/fax 61 2 4938 8134 or email: jenny@rpi.net.au for information on her classes and the pattern for the Victoria Alexandrina Christening dress.

**Pfaff American Sales Corp**
610 Winters Avenue Paramus New Jersey 07653 0566
Phone: 201 262 7221 Fax: 201 262 0696
*Pfaff sewing machines and all related products*

**Jenny Haskins Designs available from:**
Unique Creative Opportunities Pty Limited
PO Box 2156 Carlingford NSW 2118 Australia
Phone/Fax 61 2 9680 1381
Email: jenny@rpi.net.au
Web site: **www.jennyhaskins.com**
*Design Disks*
*Victorian Roses*
*Victorian Pansies*
*Victorian Scrolls and Curlicues*
*Victorian Bows and Baskets*
*Victorian Silk Panels*
*Victorian Butterflies Signature disk*
*Victorian hand painted laces*
*Victorian beads, flowers and fabrics*

**USA Distributor**
Pollards Sew Creative
1934 E Alosta Avenue, Glendora CA 91740 USA
Phone 1 626 335 2770 Fax 1 626 335 4960
Email: pollards@pollardsewcreative.com
Web site: www.pollardsewcreative.com
*USA distributor of Jenny Haskins Victorian design disks and Silk Panels*

**Berry Patch**
P.O. Box 893
Niwot, CO 80544
Phone/Fax (303) 652-1500
*Supplier of fine wired ribbons and accessories*